MURIEL MIURA'S
HOME COOKING
Hawai'i Style
Island Comfort Food at Its Best

Muriel Miura

Mutual Publishing

TO MY GRANDCHILDREN

Alissa & Stephen Ling

Library of Congress Control
Number: 2020944820

ISBN: 978-1-949307-19-1

Photo credits:
Unless otherwise credited below,
photos are from dreamstime.com
Photos ©Kaz Tanabe: pg. iv
(slippers), 3, 7-8, 12, 16, 18, 31-
32, 43-44, 48, 51, 54, 56, 57, 74,
78, 86, 89-90, 93, 97, 99-100,
103, 106, 108, 111, 113-114,
119-120, 123, 130, 137-138,
158, 161, 167, 169-170, 174, 177,
179, 181, 183, 193, 196, 199

Egg spatulas from Betty
Shimabukuro

Recipe cards on pg. xi-xii from
Muriel Miura

Cover design by Jane Gillespie
Design by Courtney Tomasu

First Printing, September 2021

Mutual Publishing, LLC
1215 Center Street, Suite 210
Honolulu, Hawaii 96816
Ph: 808-732-1709
Fax: 808-734-4094
info@mutualpublishing.com
www.mutualpublishing.com

Printed in South Korea

Other Books by the Author

As Author

Cook Japanese Hawaiian Style (Listed as Best-Seller), 1974

Hawaiian Pūpū Party Planner, 1974 • Hawaiian Potpourri, 1975

Maxi Meals for Mini Money, 1975 • Cook Japanese Hawaiian Style Volume II, 1976

New World of Cooking with Muriel, 1979 • Cooking with Hari and Muriel, 1994

From Hawai`i's Kitchen: Homemade Gifts of Sweets & Treats, 2005*

Holiday Gift Giving Recipes, 2005*

Little Hawaiian Holiday Gift-Giving Recipes, 2005* • Hawai`i's Party Food, 2007*

Japanese Cooking Hawai`i Style, 2006* • Little Hawaiian Party Food Cookbook, 2007*

Little Hawaiian Cookbooks: Tastes & Flavors of Pineapple, 2007*

What Hawai`i Likes to Eat, 2007* • Hawai`i Cooks with Spam®, 2008*

Hawai`i Cooks & Saves, 2008* • What Hawai`i Likes to Eat, Hana Hou, 2009*

Little Hawaiian Condiments Cookbook, 2011*

Little Hawaiian Japanese Cooking Hawai`i Style, 2011*

Celebrating in Hawai`i: Favorite Recipes for Holidays and Special Occasions, 2016*

Favorite Recipes from the What Hawai`i Likes to Eat Series, 2016*

Hawai`i Cooks: A Japanese Kitchen, 2017*

As Editor/Chair

Heritage of Hawai`i: Cookbook vol. I (Gasco), 1965

Heritage of Hawai`i: Cookbook vol. II (Gasco), 1970

The Legacy of the Japanese in Hawai`i: Cuisine (JCCH), 1989

Tastes & Tales of Mōili`ili (Mōili`ili Community Center), 1997*

A Tradition of Aloha Cookbook (Japanese Women's Society), 1998

Flavors of Aloha (Japanese Women's Society), 2001

Hawai`i Cooks: A Korean Kitchen, 2013* • Hawai`i Cooks: An Okinawan Kitchen, 2014*

Hawai`i Cooks: A Portuguese Kitchen, 2014* • Hawai`i Cooks: A Chinese Kitchen, 2015*

Hawai`i Cooks: A Filipino Kitchen, 2016* • A Taste of Aloha Favorites, 2019*

*Published by Mutual Publishing

Contents

MUNCHIES 'N SNACKS

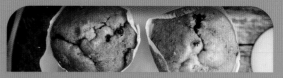

BREAD BASKET

HEARTY MAIN DISHES

BEEF

RICE & NOODLES

FAMILY FAVORITES

SALADS & SALAD DRESSINGS

SAVORY SOUPS & STEWS

EGGS 'N THINGS

SAUCES

VEGETABLES & SIDES

LAST BITE

Preface

by Betty Shimabukuro

Whenever we met up, Muriel Miura and I would compare our aches and pains, all the inconveniences creeping up on us with the passing years. "It sucks to get old," was something she said once every conversation.

Muriel always brought gifts when we met for lunch. These spatulas are from years ago but I still use them all the time.

And yet, I thought she was indestructible. That she'd always be around with her baseline belief: Food has to taste good to be good, no matter how beautiful it may appear. Showiness, fuss, bother—those things did not impress her. No nonsense. Not ever.

But Muriel did leave us, on November 7, 2020, living out her final days at her daughter's home in Baltimore. She was eighty-five.

Since then, I've been hunting for the words to memorialize someone who loomed so large throughout Hawai'i's community of home cooks. Here's what I've arrived at: She was a teacher. And she wasn't done.

This cookbook was not quite wrapped up when her health took a turn in the summer of 2020. Her daughter, Shari Ling, remembers her calling her publisher from the hospital: "She was very clear that her upcoming book will be published."

We never argued with Muriel.

Muriel's career as a teacher can be viewed in two parts, the first beginning with classes she taught for the Gas Co. in the 1960s. Her "Wiki-Wiki Kau Kau" lunchtime sessions evolved into two of the first local TV cooking shows, *Cook Japanese* and *The New World of Cooking with Muriel*, both in the 1970s.

The second part was her publishing career, which began with *Cook Japanese: Hawaiian Style* in 1974, and continued through more than twenty books that are standards on many a local kitchen shelf. *Cook Japanese* was self-published in the truest sense of the word. She used a printer who made pamphlets for the Gas Co. (it was his first book project) and did most of the sales and book delivery herself.

"I guess I had more guts than brains in those days," she once told me.

The little paperback retailed for $3.95, and it sold out several printings. It was followed by several more self-published books that helped cover her daughter's private-school tuition, then college.

Imagine Muriel in this time period: a single mom, an Asian woman, taking the spotlight, promoting herself, when few women of her background would have had the guts. Imagine what that meant to a generation of home cooks—men and women—who leaned on her teaching. Imagine what that meant to my generation of women who followed.

Leap ahead: Thirty years after the publication of *Cook Japanese*, Muriel entered a partnership with Mutual Publishing. Beginning in 2006 with *Japanese Cooking Hawai'i Style*, a slick repackaging of her modest first book, she wrote or edited more than a dozen cookbooks. She also volunteered

Muriel Kaminaka holds a first printing of her Japanese food cookbook. Some of her dishes are in front of her. (August 21, 2006 Honolulu Star-Bulletin photo by Richard Walker)

Idalia Schilling (left) and Muriel Kaminaka (right) package cookies for the Discover Moiliili Festival. They are in the Moiliili Community Center. (September 27, 2004 Honolulu Star-Bulletin photo by FL Morris)

as editor of benefit cookbooks for the Moiliili Community Center and the Japanese Women's Society, two organizations close to her heart. Our work together spanned eight cookbooks, beginning with 2007's *What Hawai'i Likes to Eat*, and continuing through the six-book series *Hawai'i Cooks*, which focused on ethnic cuisines as they have evolved in island kitchens. The throughline was always that all our recipes be practical for the home cook. She hated recipes that made you turn pages in search of another recipe for, say, a sauce to complete a dish. "Just so you can put a dot of it on the plate!" she'd say, exasperated.

Yes, Muriel was exacting. But she also found joy in food, and not just the pleasure of a good meal. What we eat connects us to a culture and a shared history, she believed, and to fully appreciate a dish is to understand its place among families and the larger community.

As is true with all great cooks and all great teachers—the best way to honor Muriel is to use her recipes. Adapt them, make them part of your family, and, by all means, pass them on. I will.

Muriel and I in 2007 at the photoshoot for What Hawai'i Likes to Eat.

Introduction

Midway through the production of *Home Cooking, Hawai'i Style*, the world changed. Like most people across the country and around the world, government guidelines were followed and many began working from home to social-distance, quarantine and shelter at home in response to the pandemic. For those like me, that meant recipe development, writing, editing and all other related activities had to be done in isolation at home.

While at home, more time is being spent by many cooking to feed families and ourselves within a limited budget. Cooking became a central rallying point with friends during this crisis, providing not just sustenance but also distraction and comfort in a time of uncertainty. Many, like myself, were busy with "isolation cooking" and quarantine baking," which explains the shortage of flour and other basic ingredients at the markets. Recipe exchanges spiked and it was nice to hear about the pantry meals and bread and pastry recipes of others.

Home Cooking, Hawai'i Style is a compilation of a treasury of "old-time favorites." Reflecting the diversity and rich cultural heritage of Hawai'i where immigrants from

all parts of the world have fostered a lifestyle that is fresh, healthy and hearty. Many recipes are classic family favorites, handed down through generations. Each has been kitchen-tested and edited for clarity, editorial uniformity and ease of preparation to fit today's lifestyle and budget.

In order to stretch the food dollar, we must use our personal resources—time and energy. It's time now to plan ahead and rediscover "good home cooking" and start preparing many things from scratch. As you cook your way through the pages of this book, it is hoped that you, too, will add your touch to the unique flavors of aloha.

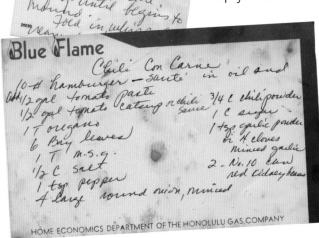

One thing is certain, cooking and baking can reset your focus and provide a respite during periods of chaos such as what we are presently experiencing. I've always wanted to work from home but did discover that working from home during "lockdown" was very challenging. The task of publishing a cookbook became somewhat problematic. However, thanks to the creative and dedicated staff at Mutual Publishing, we were able to overcome hurdles and kept things running smoothly.

In addition to recipes for delicious, affordable, kitchen-tested island favorites, I would also like to share some tips for shopping, ways to extend food, and helpful hints that will help you save time and money. You'll find that your budget will be able to afford scrumptious desserts occasionally, if you make your own.

It is hoped that you'll find lots of ideas and inspiration for cooking and saving money to keep you and your loved ones well-fed and healthy during these uncertain times and forward into the "new normal" world.

Stay safe, and keep healthy! Together, let's keep cooking!

Acknowledgments

My sincerest thanks to all those who contributed to my collection of "old time favorite" recipes. I am lucky to have so many people share food ideas with me—you have all contributed to my knowledge, my sense of flavor and sense of form. Thank you, everyone.

I am especially thankful to my daughter, Shari, who is my inspiration for everything that I do. She always shares her ideas and thoughts as well as her critiques which are greatly appreciated. Her husband, Geoffrey, is also a wonderful supporter as are my grandchildren, Alissa and Stephen who love to cook with "mom and grandma" to perpetuate the family's legacy.

My sincerest thanks to the Mutual Publishing family...this book would not have been published had it not been for their expertise, dedication, support and hard work....

> Especially to Bennett Hymer (publisher), for his friendship, faith and confidence in my work
>
> Courtney Tomasu (graphic designer), design
>
> Jane Gillespie (production director), cover design

And to you, the reader, my heartfelt thank you for embracing my work. I hope that these recipes will inspire you to be creative and use them as a guide to create your own unique dishes and memories.

Muriel Miura

Muriel Miura, CFCS

Savings Tips

Grocery prices, along with many other things, have been skyrocketing lately, especially for basic food items like beef, pork, bread, and eggs. However, even with escalating costs, there are still some options for saving money on your food bill.

Consider selecting a couple of the following strategies and give them a try. Even if you're already an expert in stretching your food dollars, you'll find that the tactics mentioned here will help you save.

HABITS TO CHANGE

- **Cook more frequently—learn to cook.** Before the pandemic, because of our busy lifestyle, many tended to prefer "meals on wheels" whereby "take-outs" and "home deliveries" were purchased for the convenience. However, it can be quite expensive. In fact, cooking was not a common skill in these days of microwavable everything and fast-food places on practically every corner. Since the pandemic, home-cooking is being rediscovered. The closer you come to made-from-scratch cooking, the less it costs to feed the family.

- **Reduce frequency.** If you currently go marketing once weekly, stretch it out to two weeks. Double the time between your shopping trips then stick to this new schedule. However, you'll probably need to do a little extra planning to get started but you'll probably find that you'll cut back on your spending.

- **Prepare less food.** If there are four of you in the family, cook for three. It's common knowledge that Americans overeat, and good cooks tend to overcook.

- **Clean out** the pantry and freezer occasionally (twice a year) and use up all the canned goods and frozen meats before they expire. Be creative and come up with all kinds of unusual fare.

CLIP 'N SHOP

- **Clip coupons** as they can help you save a ton of money—sometimes up to about 50 percent off your grocery bills. To save the most, hold coupons until that item goes on sale, which multiplies the savings.

- **Watch for sales** and build your menus around weekly specials. Look at the sale flyers you get in the mail or check the newspaper ads weekly. Also, check for websites that track the current week's sales.

CRUISING THE AISLES

- **Shop alone** and get in and out as quickly as possible as industry studies say you'll spend 10 to 40 percent more if you have your children with you and the longer you linger, the more you spend.

- **Stick to your list** and place items not on your list in that little seat at the front of the grocery cart so that when you're ready to check out, you can reassess the items and put back what you don't really need.

- **Cash-only purchases** curtail impulse purchases according to surveys.

- Plastic-packing customers tend to spend 20 to 30 percent more than the cash-only patron.

- **Carry all items** rather than grabbing a grocery cart when you only need a few things. This will prevent impulse buying.

SHOP FOR BARGAINS

- **Do comparison shopping** even between two supermarkets in different neighborhoods owned by the same company as prices can vary depending on location and competition.

- **Watch your food dollar stretch—Plan ahead, shop carefully, cook from scratch more frequently!**

Balance Your Menus

1 Color and Contrast

No monochromatic menus, please! Get good color contrasts, but make sure foods in the same course do not clash. Contrast hot dishes with cold; soft foods with crisp; bland with strong-flavored. Vary the cooking method; for instance, no completely fried dinners. Enhance a colorless dish with a sauce or colorful garnish.

2 Texture

Plan variety here too. A creamy-sauced food needs something crisp and crunchy. You might add the crunch right in the sauce, with water chestnuts, slivered nuts or celery; in the vegetable course or with a relish tray. Keep a texture contrast throughout the meal, as well as within each course. Top off a heavy meal with a light dessert, and vice versa.

3 Flavor

Include both tart and sweet, but save the very sweet for the end of the meal. One strong flavor or spiced dish is usually enough in one meal. Do not repeat flavors in the same meal (such as tomatoes, onions or nut meals).

4 Variety

Even if you can get by serving the same old standbys—don't. Hamburger can be served as Swedish meatballs, individual meat loaves, spaghetti or lasagna. Try new recipes using ingredients you know everyone likes. Combining food is an easy way to create new dishes: mix two different cans of soup together; combine carrots with scallions, peas with dill, green beans with almonds.

5 Nutrition

It's your job to see that everyone gets enough of the four basic food groups every day. Here's a nutrition tip: If you have food color contrast in daily meals and have chosen foods from each group, nutrition is taken care of. Just look at the nutrition groups. If you include each of these, you'll have a well-balanced meal and a good looking one, too.

MUNCHIES 'N SNACKS

Simple "eat-out-of-hand" munchies and snacks are popular at most gatherings today. You'll find a few of today's often requested recipes in this section that are sure to satisfy midday hunger as well as late night snacking.

Seared 'Ahi/Aku Poke

Yield: 4 to 6 servings

An easy dish to make—delicious either as a side dish or pūpū.

1 pound fresh 'ahi (yellowfin tuna) or aku (skipjack tuna), cubed
2 teaspoons fresh grated ginger root
2 teaspoons salad oil

Sauce:
3 tablespoons soy sauce
2 teaspoons sesame oil
½ cup thinly sliced sweet onion
½ cup minced green onion
¼ cup chopped limu (seaweed)
Hawaiian salt to taste
Chili pepper flakes to taste

Combine fish with ginger and salad oil; marinate 30 minutes. Sear fish in hot nonstick skillet sprayed with oil until medium rare; set aside.

Mix together soy sauce, sesame oil, onions, limu, salt and chili pepper flakes in medium bowl; add cooked fish cubes and toss gently. Refrigerate. May be served on bed of mesclun greens, if desired.

Poke
Raw Fish Appetizer

Yield: 4 to 6 servings

1 pound 'ahi (yellowfin tuna) or aku (skipjack tuna), cut into ½-inch cubes
¾ cup limu kohu (seaweed), blanched and chopped
1 tablespoon Hawaiian salt
1 Hawaiian red pepper, seeded and minced
2 teaspoons ground, roasted kukui nuts

Combine all ingredients and toss to mix. Chill before serving.

TIPS:
Following are a few tips that can be useful to anyone who plans to serve pūpū at any time.

• Serve a variety of breads, toasts and crackers. Remember that highly flavored spreads and dips are at their best when the breads or crackers are not too highly seasoned.

• Serve raw vegetables for dipping. Try carrot sticks, celery stalks, thin slices of turnip, cauliflower and the like—great flavor and the calorie-conscious will love you.

• Don't forget the ice and please have plenty of them; nothing is worse than warm drinks.

Most importantly, have a good time. The recipes here assure you of that... all great-tasting and easy. I'm sure that you will enjoy every one.

ʻAhi–Tobiko Poke

Tuna-Fish Roe Appetizer

Yield: 10 to 12 servings

3 pounds fresh ʻahi fillet, cubed
½ cup tobiko (flying fish roe)
1 pound limu kohu (seaweed), chopped
Hawaiian rock salt to taste
2 teaspoons ʻinamona (kukui nut paste)

Combine all ingredients; toss to mix well.
Chill and serve.

VARIATION:

Add 1 tablespoon hot chili or sesame
oil, ¼ cup soy sauce and 1 cup
minced green onion; toss
to combine.

Pigs in Blankets

Yield: 32 pieces

2 tablespoons Dijon mustard
1 tablespoon mayonnaise
1 tablespoon tomato ketchup
1 can (10 oz.) refrigerated flaky biscuits
2 packages (5.3 oz. each) cocktail
  frankfurters
1 egg
1 tablespoon water
2 tablespoons toasted sesame seeds

Combine mustard, mayonnaise, and tomato ketchup in a small bowl; blend well. Separate each bis cuit dough into 2 thinner ones; cut each in half to form two semicircles. Spread each semicircle with mustard mixture then top with cocktail frank. Fold dough around franks, pressing edges together to seal; place seam-side down on ungreased baking sheet. Beat together egg and water; brush over dough and sprinkle with sesame seeds. Bake. Temperature: 400°F. Time: 8 to 10 minutes or until franks are heated through and biscuits are golden brown. Best if served hot.

VARIATION:

Substitute any type of sausage for frankfurters. Portuguese sausage strips are especially 'ono.

Easy Char Siu Bao

Pork-Filled Rolls

Yield: 8 to 10

1 (10⅓ oz.) can refrigerated biscuits or dinner rolls

Filling:
1 cup char siu (sweet roast pork)
¼ cup minced green onion
½ teaspoon soy sauce
Dash of pepper

2 tablespoons salad oil

Combine Filling ingredients and mix thoroughly. Place 1 table spoon filling in center of each circle of dough. Pinch edges together to seal. Brush tops with salad oil. Steam, seam side down, in waxed paper-lined steamer for 15 to 20 minutes.

TIP:
Rolls may also be baked at 375°F for 10 minutes or until golden.

Pizza

Yield: 6 servings

2 cups Basic Biscuit Mix (see page 22)
½ cup milk
1 pound pork sausage
¼ teaspoon thyme
¼ teaspoon garlic powder
½ teaspoon oregano
2 1-pound cans whole tomatoes, drained
1 cup shredded cheese

Combine biscuit mix with milk to make a dough. Turn onto a floured board or pastry cloth and knead 5 to 6 times. Roll out dough into a 10 x 12 inch rectangle. Place on a greased baking sheet. Roll edges of dough to hold in filling.

Brown pork sausage and drain excess fat. Add seasonings. Spread tomatoes on dough, cover with cheese, then top with sausage. Bake at 450°F for 10 to 15 minutes or until cheese melts. Serve hot.

Gau Gee with Sweet and Sour Sauce

Yield: about 4 dozen

Filling:
½ pound ground pork
½ pound shrimp, shelled, cleaned and minced
1 teaspoon ginger juice
½ teaspoon salt
2 tablespoons soy sauce
1 tablespoon sesame oil
1 tablespoon cooking wine
2 tablespoons chopped celery

Liquid canola oil for deep frying
1 package won ton pi (flour wrappers)

Sauce:
⅓ cup sugar
¼ cup soy sauce
2 tablespoons cooking wine
2 tablespoons tomato ketchup
3 tablespoons vinegar
2 tablespoons cornstarch
1 cup water

Mix filling ingredients in a bowl. Place 1 teaspoon of filling on a won ton pi. Fold in half and seal edges with mixture of cornstarch and water. Deep fry in 365°F oil.

Hawaiian Jambles

Yield: about 4 quarts

1 cup butter or margarine
½ teaspoon onion salt
½ teaspoon celery salt
½ teaspoon garlic salt
1 tablespoon Worcestershire sauce
10 drops liquid hot sauce
½ box (7 oz.) square rice cereal
½ box (7 oz.) round oat cereal
1 box (7½ oz.) very thin pretzel sticks
1 can (6½ oz.) macadamia nuts

Place cereals, pretzels, and nuts in large baking pan. Melt butter or margarine; add seasonings and pour seasoning mixture over cereals and stir until all ingredients are coated. Bake, stirring every 20 to 30 minutes. Temperature: 250°F. Time: 1 to 2 hours or until crisp. Cool thoroughly and store in airtight container.

VARIATIONS:

- Oriental-Style: Prepare as above except substitute 3 tablesoons soy sauce for Worcestershire sauce. Add 2 teaspoons Chinese five spice powder to butter mixture and add one 5-ounce can chow mein noodles and 1 cup bite-size fish-shape crackers to cereal mixture.

- Cajun Style: Prepare as above except increase hot pepper sauce to 1 tablespoon and substitute pecan halves for macadamia nuts.

TIP:
Salting nuts: To 1 cup nuts in pan, add 1
teaspoon salad oil; stir. Brown at 325°F
or 350°F, stirring often.
Drain and salt.

Spicy Teri Chicken Wings

Yield: 6 to 8 servings

You'll enjoy these hot, spicy chicken wings seasoned with soy sauce, sugar, ginger and "heated" with hot red chilis.

2 pounds chicken wing drumettes
2½ tablespoons canola oil
¼ cup soy sauce
2 tablespoons mirin (sweet rice wine)
¼ cup sugar
1 teaspoon chili oil or 1 small dried red chili
2 small slices fresh ginger
1 clove garlic, minced
½ cup minced green onion
1 cup water

Rinse chicken and pat dry. Heat oil in wide skillet over high heat. Add chicken, a few pieces at a time; cook, turning as needed to brown on all sides. Return all chicken to pan, and then add soy sauce, mirin, sugar, chili oil, ginger, garlic, onions and water. Bring to a boil. Then reduce heat, cover, and simmer 15 to 20 minutes or until meat near bone is no longer pink. Uncover and continue cooking, turning chicken occasionally, until sauce is thick enough to coat chicken pieces, about 10 minutes. Serve warm or at room temperature.

Shrimp Cups

Yield: 36 pieces

A cookbook of favorite recipes from Hawai'i wouldn't be complete without using won ton wrappers. Here's a unique way of using one of Hawai'i's favorite wrappers.

36 won ton wrappers

<u>Filling:</u>
½ pound tiny cooked bay shrimps
¼ cup finely minced green onion
¼ cup finely minced onion
3 tablespoons mayonnaise
2 tablespoons sour cream
1 teaspoon curry powder
1 teaspoon lemon juice
Dash of salt
Dash of cayenne, optional

<u>Garnishes:</u>
Shredded coconut
Chopped cilantro or parsley

Prepare won ton cups by pressing wrappers into nonstick 1½-inch muffin tins. Bake. Temperature: 350°F. Time: 8 to 10 minutes or until crisp and golden. Cool before filling. If won ton cups are made in advance, store airtight up to 3 days.

To prepare filling, combine all ingredients in a bowl; stir until well mixed. Using slotted spoon, scoop shrimp mixture into won ton cups just before serving. Sprinkle each with coconut and cilantro or parsley to garnish. Keep refrigerated.

VARIATION:
Won ton cups may be filled with any type of filling of your choice.

TIP:
To tint coconut, mix 1 tablespoon water and desired amount of food coloring in a quart jar. Add about 1 cup shredded coconut. Cover jar and shake until color is evenly distributed. Spread coconut on paper towel to dry before using.

Fresh Tomato Salsa

Yield: about 3½ cups

This fresh tomato-based salsa adds excitement to everything it touches—taco chips, fish, eggs and meat. It is a staple of southwestern cooking plus you have a delicious dip that's low in calories.

3 medium tomatoes, seeded and chopped
½ cup minced green onion
¼ cup chopped green bell pepper
3 tablespoons lime juice
2½ tablespoons chopped fresh cilantro
1 tablespoon finely chopped jalapeño chilis
½ teaspoon salt
2 cloves garlic, minced

Mix all ingredients and serve with tortilla chips, crackers or vegetables.

Italian Nachos

Yield: varies

Nachos always taste so good—it's perfect for any gathering.

1 package Italian smoked sausage, thinly sliced
1 bag tortilla chips
Monterey Jack or taco-flavored cheese
Sour cream for garnish, optional

Place thinly sliced sausage on tortilla chips. Top with cheese and broil until cheese melts. Top with sour cream, if desired.

Gyoza
Pork Pot Stickers

Yield: approximately 3 dozen

The pork filling for this popular dumpling may be substituted with ground chicken. This dish is often served as a side with ramen or other noodle dishes.

Filling:
¼ pound ground pork
½ pound ground beef
1 egg, beaten
2 dried shiitake (mushrooms), softened in water and minced
¼ teaspoon salt
1 tablespoon shoyu
1 tablespoon mirin (sweet rice wine)
¼ teaspoon sesame seed oil
2 tablespoons minced green onion or chives
1 cup finely minced cabbage, optional

3 dozen gyoza wrappers or won ton pi
1 quart canola oil for frying

Combine filling ingredients and mix thoroughly.

To make a pot sticker:
Fill each gyoza wrapper with 1 tablespoon filling mixture. Moisten edges of wrapper. Fold in half and flute edges to seal.

Fry in oil heated to 365°F for 1 to 2 minutes or until golden brown. Gyoza may also be steam-fried for 20 to 30 minutes instead. Drain on absorbent paper and serve with purchased ponzu or shoyu.

California Dip

Yield: about 2 cups

I've been told that all those great cocktail dips of today started with this recipe. It has been popular since about 1954.

1 envelope (1¾ oz.) onion soup mix
2 cups (16 oz.) sour cream

In a small bowl blend onion soup mix with sour cream; chill. Serve with a variety of toasts and crackers or try carrot sticks, celery stalks, thin slices of turnip, cauliflower, and the like—great flavor and the calorie conscious will love you.

VARIATIONS:

• California Vegetable Dip: Add 1 green pepper, chopped; 1 tomato, chopped; and 2 teaspoons chili powder.

• Blue Cheese Dip: Add ¼ pound blue cheese, crumbled and ¼ cup finely chopped macadamia nuts or walnuts.

• Shrimp Dip: Add 1 cup finely chopped cooked shrimp and ¼ cup ketchup.

• Clam Dip: Add 1 can (7½ oz.) minced clams, drained and 2 tablespoons chili sauce.

Spinach Rolls

Yield: about 6 dozen pieces

2 packages (10 oz. size) frozen chopped spinach, thawed
1 cup sour cream
1 cup mayonnaise
½ bottle (3 oz. size) bacon bits
1 package (1 oz.) ranch-style salad dressing mix
½ cup chopped green onions
¼ cup chopped water chestnuts
10 (8-inch) flour tortillas

Squeeze moisture from spinach. In a bowl, combine spinach, sour cream, mayonnaise, bacon bits, dressing mix, onions, and water chestnuts; mix well. Spread evenly over tortillas and roll tortillas tightly. Cover with plastic wrap and chill overnight. Slice into 1-inch pieces.

Pipikaula
Beef Jerky

Yield: About 3 pounds

**4 pounds flank steak, cut into 2-inch
wide strips**

Marinade:
1 cup soy sauce
½ cup sake (rice wine) or dry sherry
2 teaspoons liquid smoke
3 tablespoons sugar
2 teaspoons salt
¼ teaspoon pepper
1 piece ginger root, minced
2 cloves garlic, minced
**2 Hawaiian red peppers, seeded and
minced**

Combine all marinade ingredients; mix
well and marinate meat for 24 hours in
refrigerator, turning several times. Drain
meat and arrange on racks placed on
baking sheets. Dry meat in oven at 200°F
for 7 to 8 hours until meat is the texture of
"jerky." Meat may be stored for 5 days in
the refrigerator or in the freezer for 6 to 8
months. To serve, slice diagonally.

Boiled Peanuts

Yield: 1 pound

1 pound raw peanuts in shell
½ cup Hawaiian rock salt
3 to 4 star anise
1 teaspoon sugar

Place peanuts in pot with water to cover.
Add remaining ingredients; bring to a boil.
Cover and simmer for 1 to 1½ hours or
until peanuts are tender but firm.

Spicy Mixed Nuts

Yield: about 2 cups

1 tablespoon canola oil
2 cups assorted unsalted nuts (macadamia,
    almonds, pecans, walnuts, peanuts)
2 tablespoons sugar
1 teaspoon paprika
½ teaspoon chili powder
½ teaspoon curry powder
½ teaspoon ground cumin
½ teaspoon coriander
½ teaspoon black pepper
¼ teaspoon salt

Heat oil in large skillet over
moderate heat; cook and stir nuts in
hot oil 2 to 3 minutes or until browned.
Combine remaining ingredients in a small
bowl; sprinkle over nuts; stir to coat evenly.
Heat additional 1 to 2 minutes. Drain nuts on
absorbent paper. Delicious warm. Completely
cool before storing in airtight container.

VARIATION:
Curried Mixed Nuts:
Prepare as directed
above except use
2½ teaspoons curry
powder and ½
teaspoon garlic salt
only for seasoning;
do not use other
seasonings listed
above.

Lumpia

Filipino-Style Spring Rolls

Yield: about 5 dozen

This finger food is similar to the Chinese egg roll and Southeast Asian spicy rolls. The sweet-sour dipping sauce makes this dish very special.

Filling:

1 pound lean ground beef
1 clove garlic, minced
½ cup minced green onion
¼ cup minced water chestnuts
¼ cup minced mushrooms
½ cup green beans, minced
1 tablespoon soy sauce
½ teaspoon salt
¼ teaspoon pepper
1 egg, slightly beaten

1 package lumpia wrappers (spring roll shells)
1 quart canola oil for frying

Lumpia Sauce:

⅓ cup soy sauce
3 tablespoons fresh lemon juice

Brown ground beef with garlic; drain excess oil. Add remaining Filling ingredients and sauté until meat is done. Cool. Place 2 tablespoons filling about 2 inches from nearest edge of each wrapper. Fold edge of wrapper over filling; fold left and right sides toward the center to enclose filling in envelope fashion. Roll toward open end. Moisten edge with water and seal. Deep-fry in oil heated to 365°F for 2 to 3 minutes or until golden on all sides. Drain on absorbent paper; cut each diagonally into thirds. Serve with Lumpia Sauce by combining soy sauce with lemon juice.

Wikiwiki Pūpū

Following are some suggestions for pūpū that can be "made-in-a-minute."

- Marinate cooked shrimp in Italian dressing for a couple of hours in the refrigerator. Drain and arrange on picks with pitted ripe olives.
- Spread thin ham slices with whipped cream cheese; roll up and chill. Cut into 1-inch pieces.
- Combine flaked crabmeat with enough mayonnaise to moisten; season lightly with curry powder and serve as a spread with melba toast.
- Spread one 8-ounce package cream cheese with mango chutney and serve with crackers.
- Simmer cocktail sausages, ham or luncheon meat cubes in teriyaki sauce. Keep warm in chafing dish or over warmer.
- Spread thin slices of French bread with soft butter or margarine; top with shredded Mozzarella cheese. Heat in oven at 350°F until cheese melts.
- Split leftover biscuits or croissants and top with shredded cheese and chopped chilis. Broil or bake until cheese melts.
- Brush tortilla chips with melted butter or margarine and sprinkle with sugar-cinnamon. Bake until bubbly; cool slightly before serving.

Teriyaki Meat Sticks

Yield: about 18 to 20

1 pound beef, cut in 4-inch strips

Marinade:
½ cup brown sugar, packed
½ cup soy sauce
¼ cup sake (rice wine) or sherry
1 clove garlic, crushed
1-inch piece fresh ginger root, crushed

**Bamboo skewers, soaked in water 45
  minutes before using**

Thread meat strips on skewers by weaving
skewer in and out; set aside.

Combine Marinade ingredients in
resealable bag; mix well. Add beef sticks;
marinate 15 to 30 minutes. Broil, turning
once and basting occasionally until
desired doneness, about 3 to 4 minutes.
Serve hot.

BREAD BASKET

The smell of bread baking is one of the most delicious and inviting aromas! This section features a variety of bread recipes from biscuits, muffins, quick breads, yeast breads and more. Once you delve into the world of baking breads, you'll find that the experience is not only fulfilling but simply delicious as well!

Basic White Bread

Yield: 2 loaves

5½ to 6½ cups flour
3 tablespoons sugar
2 teaspoons salt
1 package active dry yeast
1½ cups water
½ cup milk
3 tablespoons butter or margarine

In a large bowl, mix 2 cups flour, sugar, salt and undissolved yeast.

Combine water, milk and butter or margarine. Heat over low heat until liquids are warm. Gradually add to dry ingredients and beat 2 minutes at medium speed with mixer, scraping bowl occasionally. Add ¾ cup flour or enough flour to make a thick batter. Beat at high speed for 2 minutes, scraping bowl occasionally. Stir in enough flour to make a soft dough. Turn out onto a lightly floured board; knead until smooth and elastic, about 8 to 10 minutes.

Place dough in a lightly greased bowl, turning once to grease top. Cover bowl with clean cloth and let rise in warm place (about 80°F) until doubled in bulk, about 1 hour.

Punch dough down; turn out onto lightly floured board. Cover; let rest 15 minutes. Divide dough in half and shape into loaves. Place in 2 greased 9 x 5-inch loaf pans, seam side down. Cover; let rise until doubled in bulk, about 1 hour.

Bake at 400°F for 25 to 30 minutes. Remove from pans and cool on wire racks.

VARIATION:

Cinnamon Bread: Divide Basic White Bread in half after first rising; roll out into 12 x 8-inch rectangles and brush surface lightly with softened or melted butter or margarine. Mix ⅓ cup sugar with ⅓ cup cinnamon; sprinkle half evenly over top of each rectangle. Roll tightly from the 8-inch side, as for jelly roll. Pinch edges firmly to seal. Place loaves, seam side down, in greased 8½ x 4½ x 2½-inch loaf pans. Cover; let rise in warm place until doubled in bulk, about 1 hour.

Bake at 375°F for 30 to 45 minutes or until loaves sound hollow when tapped. Remove from pans and cool on wire racks. Drizzle with icing, if desired.

TIP:
The ideal temperature for the rising of yeast dough is 80°F to 85°F, which is about 10°F warmer than ordinary room temperature.

Whole Wheat Bread

Yield: 2 loaves

The flavor of this bread is sweet, wholesome and nutty. This is a perfect beginning loaf using whole wheat flour.

9¾ cups whole wheat flour
3½ teaspoons salt
2 packages active dry yeast
1½ cups milk
1½ cups water
½ cup honey
6 tablespoons butter or margarine

In large mixer bowl, combine 3 cups of the flour, salt and yeast. Combine milk, water, honey and butter in saucepan; cook over low heat, stirring occasionally, until mixture is warm enough to dissolve yeast. Add slowly to flour mixture; beat 2 minutes at medium speed. Add 3 more cups of the flour; beat 2 more minutes at high speed. Stir in enough additional flour to make a soft dough. Place dough on lightly floured board; cover and let rest 10 minutes. Knead in remaining flour until dough is smooth and elastic, about 7 to 10 minutes. Place dough in greased bowl, turning dough to grease top. Cover; let rise until dough is doubled. Grease two 9 x 5-inch loaf pans; set aside.

Punch down dough and on a lightly floured board, divide in half. Shape each half into a loaf; place in prepared pans, seam side down. Cover; let rise again until dough is doubled. Bake. Temperature: 375°F. Time: 35 minutes or until loaves sound hollow when tapped. Remove from pans and cool on wire racks.

Basic Biscuit Mix

Yield: 11 cups

8 cups flour
2½ teaspoons salt
¼ cup double-acting baking powder
¼ cup sugar, optional
2 teaspoons cream of tartar, optional
2 cups shortening

Sift together dry ingredients; cut in shortening until mixture resembles coarse crumbs. The Basic Biscuit Mix is now ready to use or store in a closed canister on your pantry shelf or in your refrigerator.

VARIATIONS:

- Baking Powder Biscuits:
  (Yield: about 8 biscuits/variations)

  2 cups purchased or Basic Biscuit Mix
  ½ cup milk

  Make a well in the biscuit mix. Add milk and stir with a fork. Turn onto a lightly floured board or pastry cloth and knead 5 to 6 times. Pat or roll to desired thickness; cut with floured cutter. Place on greased cookie sheet. Bake. Temperature: 450°F. Time: 12 to 15 minutes.

- Bacon Biscuits: 3 slices of bacon in small pieces. Pan-fry. Drain. Add to dry ingredients before adding milk.

- Cheese Diamond Biscuits: Cut Baking Powder Biscuit dough into diamond shapes. Sprinkle with ¾ cup shredded sharp cheese.

- Marmalade Drop Biscuits: After Baking Powder Biscuit dough has been dropped on baking sheet, make a small dent on top of each. Add a dab of orange marmalade.

- Orange Biscuits: Substitute 1 tablespoon orange juice and 1 tablespoon grated orange peel for part of milk. Place juice and peel in cup. Pour in milk to the ½-cup mark. Add 1½ tablespoons sugar to dry ingredients.

- Prosciutto Biscuits: Add ¼ cup finely chopped prosciutto to dry ingredients before adding milk.

Cinnamon Pinwheels

Yield: 8 rolls

Cinnamon swirl pinwheels are always enjoyed for breakfast. Serve them hot, right out of the oven!

2 cups Basic Biscuit Mix (see page 22)
½ cup milk
1 tablespoon melted butter or margarine
2 tablespoons sugar
¼ teaspoon cinnamon

Make a well in the biscuit mix. Add milk and stir with a fork. Turn onto a lightly floured board or pastry cloth and knead 5 to 6 times. Roll out dough into an 8 x 12-inch rectangle. Spread with butter or margarine. Sprinkle with sugar mixed with cinnamon. Roll up like jelly roll. Cut into 1-inch slices. Place cut side down on a greased baking sheet. Bake. Temperature: 450°F. Time: 15 minutes.

VARIATION:

Banana Pinwheels: Follow directions for Cinnamon Pinwheels except add banana slices, sprinkled with 1 tablespoon lemon juice, before rolling up.

Mango Bread

Yield: 1 loaf

Who can resist yet another recipe for this delicious fruit? This bread freezes well and may be served for breakfast or as a dessert.

2 cups flour
2 teaspoons baking soda
2½ teaspoons ground cinnamon
1¼ cups sugar
½ cup chopped nut
2¼ cups chopped ripe mangoes
¾ cup salad oil
3 eggs, beaten
1½ teaspoons vanilla

Whisk together flour, baking soda and cinnamon in large mixing bowl. Stir in sugar and nuts; add remaining ingredients and mix well. Pour into greased 9 x 5 x 3-inch loaf pan. Bake. Temperature: 350°F. Time: 60 to 75 minutes or until done.

VARIATION:

Add ½ cup grated coconut and ½ cup raisins, if desired.

Banana Bread

Yield: 1 loaf, 8½ x 4½ inches

Mrs. Margaret Inouye, wife of late U.S. Senator Daniel Inouye, shared this recipe with me over lunch in the at the Senate Dining Room of the Nation's Capitol in 1989.

2 cups sifted enriched flour
2 teaspoons baking powder
¾ teaspoon salt
½ teaspoon baking soda
1 cup granulated sugar
½ cup shortening
2 eggs
1 cup mashed bananas
1 teaspoon lemon juice
1 cup macadamia nuts, chopped

Sift dry ingredients together. Add shortening, eggs, and ½ cup bananas. Stir to combine ingredients, then beat 2 minutes at medium speed with electric mixer or 300 strokes by hand. Add remaining bananas and lemon juice. Beat 2 minutes more. Fold in ¾ cup nuts. Pour into greased, 8½ x 4½ lined loaf pan. Sprinkle ¼ cup nuts over batter. Bake at 350°F for 50 to 60 minutes or until done.

Fry Bread

Yield: 8 fry breads

1½ cups all-purpose flour
1½ teaspoons baking powder
¼ teaspoon kosher salt
Pinch of red pepper flakes
1 cup warm water
½ cup vegetable oil, divided
Yellow cornmeal

Combine flour, baking powder, salt, and pepper flakes in a bowl. Stir in water and knead dough until soft, adjusting flour and water as necessary. Cover dough and let rest 15 to 20 minutes.

Heat ¼ cup oil in a nonstick skillet over medium-high. Divide dough into 8 pieces and roll each on a surface dusted with cornmeal into a 4- to 5-inch round. Fry rounds in hot oil until puffy and golden on bottom, then flip and fry on the other side until golden, adding more oil as needed. Serve the fry bread warm.

Portuguese Sweet Bread

Yield: Four 9 x 5 x 3-inch loaves

2 packages active dry yeast
½ cup warm potato water
3 tablespoons sugar
1 cup mashed potatoes
⅛ teaspoon ground ginger
½ cup milk
1½ teaspoons salt
6 eggs
1¾ cups sugar
½ cup butter or margarine, melted
8 to 10 cups flour

Dissolve yeast in potato wafer. Stir in the sugar, potatoes, and ginger. Cover; let rise until doubled. Scald milk; add soil and cool lo lukewarm. In small bowl of electric mixer, beat eggs; gradually beat in the 1 ¾ cups sugar. Stir into yeast mixture. Add butter and mix well. Stir in 2 cups of the flour, then the milk. Add 2 more cups of the flour; beat 5 minutes. Stir in enough remaining flour lo make stiff dough. Place on lightly floured board and knead in remaining flour until dough is smooth and elastic, about 8 to 10 minutes. Place in greased bowl, turning to grease top of dough. Cover; let rise until dough is doubled. Grease four 9 x 5 x 3-inch loaf pans. Punch down dough and, on a lightly floured board, divide info fourths. Shape each fourth into a loaf; place in prepared pans. Cover; let rise until doubled. Bake at 325°F for 45 minutes or until golden brown and done.

Muffins Supreme

Yield: 12 large muffins

Everyone loves fresh muffins. They are great for breakfast, fantastic for parties or just a delicious snack. You'll enjoy using this simple master recipe as you can make a variety of muffins, by simply adding your choice of flavoring, fruit, chocolate and nuts.

Master Batter:
3½ cups flour
4 teaspoons baking powder
½ teaspoon baking soda
½ teaspoon salt
1⅓ cups sugar
10 tablespoons unsalted butter, melted and cooled slightly
1 cup whole milk, at room temperature
1 cup sour cream, at room temperature
2 large eggs, at room temperature
1 large egg yolk, at room temperature

Sift together flour, baking powder, baking soda and salt in large mixing bowl; mix together well. In medium mixing bowl, whisk together sugar, butter, milk, sour cream, eggs and egg yolk until well combined.

Make a well in the center of the dry ingredients; pour wet ingredients into the dry and fold gently just until dry ingredients are moistened (the batter will be lumpy) with still a few streaks of dry flour. Choose add-ins from lists (next page); sprinkle them into the batter and fold them in until just combined. Do not over mix.

Spoon batter into sprayed and lined 12-cup standard (2¾ inches across and about 1 inch deep) muffin tins distributing the batter evenly. The batter should mound higher than the rim of the cups by about ¾ inch. Bake. Temperature: 350°F. Time: 30 to 35 minutes or until golden brown and muffins spring back when middle is pressed lightly. (The muffin tops will probably meld together.) Let cool on a rack 15 to 20 minutes. Glaze, if desired. Best served immediately.

Glaze:
3 cups confectioners' sugar
6 tablespoons flavoring or water (lemon, orange or pineapple juice)

Combine sugar with flavoring or water; mix well and brush on muffins with pastry brush. Let stand 20 to 30 minutes to set glaze.

MUFFINS SUPREME VARIATIONS:

FLAVORINGS
(Choose 1 or 2)
Almond extract
  (½ teaspoon)
Ground cinnamon
  (½ teaspoon)
Coconut (¾ cup) flaked
  or shredded
Lemon zest, grated
  (2 teaspoons)
Orange zest, grated
  (2 teaspoons)
Vanilla extract
  (1 teaspoon)

FRUIT & CHOCOLATE
(Choose 1 or 2, 1 cup total)
Apricot halves fresh or
  canned, chopped
Bananas, sliced thinly
Blueberries, fresh or
  frozen
Chocolate bits
Cranberries, fresh
  or frozen, coarsely
  chopped

NUTS
(Choose one)
Pecan pieces, toasted
Sliced almonds, toasted
Walnut pieces, toasted
Macadamia nut bits

Dutch Baby Oven Pancake

Yield: 1 to 2 servings

This Dutch Baby German pancake is simply delicious! When baked, it puffs up incredibly.

2 tablespoons margarine or butter
2 large eggs
½ cup flour
½ cup milk
¼ teaspoon salt, optional
Powdered sugar and lemon juice or sliced fruit, if desired

Heat oven to 400°F. Melt margarine or butter in 9-inch pie pan in oven; brush melted margarine or butter on sides of pan. In medium bowl, beat eggs slightly with wire whisk or hand beater; beat in flour and milk. Pour into pie pan. Bake for 25 to 30 minutes or until puffy and golden brown. Serve immediately with lemon juice and powdered sugar or fresh fruits.

VARIATION:
Apple Oven Pancake: Sprinkle 2 tablespoons packed brown sugar and ½ teaspoon ground cinnamon evenly over melted margarine in pie pan. Arrange 1 medium baking apple, peeled and thinly sliced over sugar; pour batter over and bake 30 to 35 minutes. Immediately loosen edge of pancake and invert onto heatproof serving plate and serve hot.

Lavosh
Armenian Flatbread

Yield: about 3 dozen rounds

Lavosh is a puffy flatbread that is crisper than pita bread. Eat lavosh plain or with butter and it is an excellent accompaniment to soups, salads and entrees.

2¾ cups flour
¼ cup sugar
½ teaspoon salt
½ teaspoon baking soda
½ cup butter
1 cup buttermilk
Poppy and sesame seeds

Blend all dry ingredients together. Cut butter into flour mixture until texture is like cornmeal. Add buttermilk and mix until dough is sticky. Shape dough into 1-inch balls. Roll out each ball on lightly floured surface into very thin 4 to 5 inch circles. Press tops and bottoms of rounds with sesame and/or poppy seeds. Bake. Temperature: 400°F. Time: 4 to 5 minutes or until golden.

> **TIP:**
> Buttermilk and sour milk are interchangeable. If you have neither, here's how to make 1 cupful. Put 1 to 2 tablespoons vinegar into a cup, and fill the rest of the cup with sweet milk.

No-Knead Pan Rolls

Yield: about 2 dozen

Such an easy roll to make that you'll find yourself baking these rolls often.

1 cup lukewarm water
⅓ cup melted butter or margarine
1 tablespoon sugar
2 teaspoons salt
2 packages active dry yeast
1 egg, beaten
3½ cups flour, sifted
¼ cup melted butter or margarine

Stir to combine first 4 ingredients; add yeast. Blend in egg and add flour, mixing dough until well-blended. Roll out onto floured surface and place in greased 9 x 12-inch pan. Cut dough into 1 x 4-inch rectangles; brush cut sides with melted butter or margarine. Let rise in warm place until doubled in bulk, about 30 to 45 minutes. Bake. Temperature: 425°F. Time: 20 minutes.

Irish Soda Bread

Yield: 1 loaf

1⅔ cups flour
3 tablespoons sugar
1 teaspoon baking powder
½ teaspoon baking soda
½ teaspoon salt
½ cup raisins or currants
2 teaspoons caraway seeds
1 large egg, beaten
¾ cup buttermilk
¼ cup unsalted butter, melted

Combine flour, sugar, baking powder, baking soda, and salt in large bowl; whisk together then stir in raisins or currants and caraway seeds. In separate bowl, beat together butter milk and butter. Add the liquid mixture to the dry mixture and stir just until dry ingredients are moistened. The batter will be stiff but sticky. Scrape batter onto baking sheet to form mound 6 to 7 inches in diameter or scrape into greased loaf pan; spread evenly. Using a sharp knife, slash large "X" about 12 inches deep into top of batter. Bake at 350°F 25 to 30 minutes on baking sheet or 45 to 60 minutes in loaf pan or until golden brown.

Cornbread Supreme

Yield: 6 to 9 servings

A breakfast bread that is delicious with whipped honey butter—or try some with tropical flavored jam or jelly.

2 cups purchased or Basic Biscuit Mix (see page 22)
½ cup yellow cornmeal
½ teaspoon baking powder
½ teaspoon baking soda
1 cup sugar
¾ cup butter or margarine, melted
1 cup milk
3 eggs, beaten

Combine all dry ingredients in large mixing bowl. Make a well in the center of dry mixture; add beaten mixture of butter, milk and eggs; stir just until batter is smooth. Do not overbeat. Pour batter into nonstick or greased 9 x 13-inch pan. Bake. Temperature: 350°F. Time: 25 to 30 minutes or until wooden pick inserted in center comes out clean. Serve warm or at room temperature with whipped butter.

VARIATIONS:
- Herb Cornbread: Add 1 teaspoon herb of choice to batter.
- Cheese Cornbread: Add ½ cup shredded sharp cheddar cheese to batter.
- Extra Rich: Increase butter or margarine to 1 cup (2 blocks).

Scones

Yield: about 15

Who's concerned about calories when there are hot scones? Enjoy them but do practice moderation when eating them. Truly yummy!

1¾ cups flour
¼ cup sugar
2½ teaspoons baking powder
¼ teaspoon salt
⅓ cup butter or margarine
1 egg, beaten
½ cup raisins or currants
¼ cup diced cream cheese
4 to 6 tablespoons half-and-half
1 egg, beaten

Combine flour, sugar, baking powder and salt in large mixing bowl; mix until well blended. Cut butter or margarine into dry ingredients until mixture resembles fine crumbs. Stir in 1 egg, currants or raisins, cream cheese and just enough half-and-half so dough leaves side of bowl.

Turn dough onto lightly floured surface; knead lightly about 10 times. Roll or pat to ½ inch thick; cut with floured biscuit cutter, or pat dough into rectangle and cut into diamond shapes with sharp knife. Place on ungreased baking sheet. Brush tops with remaining egg. Bake. Temperature: 400°F. Time: 10 to 12 minutes or until golden brown. Serve immediately with butter and preserves, if desired.

TIP:
One pound of butter equals 2 cups. One stick (¼ pound) equals ½ cup.

HEARTY MAIN DISHES

The mainstay of our favorite meals has always been meat. According to the U.S. Department of Agriculture, the term meat refers to the Muscle of cattle, pigs, sheep and goats with beef and pork prevailing In North America as the meat of choice.

Over time, changes in economic conditions and taste may have caused dips and peaks in the popularity of various meats, however, meat still remains the most common source of protein in our diets. The recipes for beef, pork, seafood and poultry are presented separately in this section.

The production and consumption of meat has changed drastically over recent years with growing health concerns and the meat industry has responded accordingly. Animals are bred for leaner meat and meat cuts are trimmed more closely at the supermarkets. Also, with more than sixty cuts of beef alone to choose from, shopping for a piece of beef alone can be a daunting experience.

The focus on cooking and preparing meals today is about healthy cuisine. Now, instead of low-calorie recipes, the trend today is on delicious meals centered around healthy, nutritious, fresh ingredients.

This section offers you recipes for an exciting variety of tantalizing comfort foods utilizing some less expensive cuts of meats to help trim your budget. Read the recipes carefully, tweak it to your liking and get cooking!

BEEF

Beef has always been the mainstay of our favorite meals—be it meatloaf, kahl bi, loco moco or beef stew. While cherishing old classic dishes, people are also interested in branching out in new directions, however, without any doubt, beef is here to stay!

Never Fail Roast Beef

Yield: varies

Does this recipe work? Yes it does. Once you try it, you'll never go back to the traditional way of roasting beef. For a well seasoned roast, I prefer using seasoned Hawaiian salt.

Beef rib roast or cross rib roast, any size
Seasoned Hawaiian or Kosher salt to taste
Cracked pepper to taste

Season roast generously once the roast beef reaches room temperature. Place roast on rack in a shallow roasting pan. Roast. Temperature: 400°F. Time: 1 hour. Turn oven off. **DO NOT OPEN OVEN DOOR.** Let roast rest 3 hours in oven for initial phase of roasting. (Internal temperature 165°F). 20 minutes before serving, turn oven to 300°F and cook roast. 20 minutes to reheat. Serve with purchased horseradish or au jus.

Beef Stroganoff

Yield: 5 to 6 servings

This is a great make-ahead dish that can be elegant. The beef mixture can be prepared in advance and refrigerated or frozen. To serve, cook the noodles, if used, while reheating the meat and sauce; stir in the sour cream just before serving.

1½ pounds boneless top round or chuck steak, cut into 1½-inch cubes
½ cup flour
⅓ cup canola oil
8 ounces mushrooms, cleaned and sliced
2 tablespoons butter or margarine
1 small clove garlic, minced
1 cup chopped onion
1½ cups beef broth
½ cup dry sherry
2 tablespoons ketchup
1 teaspoon salt
½ teaspoon pepper
1 cup sour cream or plain yogurt
Buttered egg noodles or steamed rice
Chopped fresh dill, optional

Dredge beef cubes in flour, then sear in 3 tablespoons hot oil in a large pot over high heat until browned, 1 minute per side. Remove from pot; add remaining 2 tablespoons oil and reduce heat to medium. Add mushrooms and sauté until golden, stirring frequently; remove from pan. Melt butter or margarine in pot; add garlic and onion; sauté until onion is tender, about 2 minutes. Stir in broth, sherry, ketchup, salt and pepper; cook 1 minute. Return beef and mushrooms to pot and bring to a boil; reduce heat and simmer over low heat 45 to 60 minutes or until beef is tender. Stir in sour cream; heat until hot. Serve over hot cooked noodles or steamed rice. Garnish with dollop of sour cream and chopped fresh dill, if desired.

Swiss Steak

Yield: 4 to 6 servings

2 pounds round steak, 1-inch thick
½ cup flour
2 teaspoons salt
½ teaspoon pepper
2 tablespoons canola oil
1 medium onion, sliced
½ cup carrot, diced
½ cup celery, diced
2 cans (8 oz. each) tomato sauce

Cut meat into serving pieces. Combine flour, salt and pepper. Pound into meat. Brown on both sides in hot oil. Add onion, carrot, celery and tomato sauce. Cover and simmer 1½ to 2 hours or until meat is tender.

Basic Hamburger Mix

Yield: 4 to 6 servings

Hamburgers served hot off the grill can't be beat! Try some of the variations as you'll find them equally appealing.

1 pound lean ground beef
1 teaspoon salt
Dash of pepper
1 egg
½ cup chopped onion
¼ cup milk
¼ cup bread crumbs
¼ cup tomato ketchup

Combine all ingredients and mix thoroughly. Form into 4 to 6 patties. Pan fry or broil. Serve with desired sauce or as is.

VARIATIONS:

Mexican Burgers Sauce
1 can (8 oz.) tomato sauce
1 small can kidney beans, drained
¼ cup chopped onion
2 teaspoons chili powder
½ cup shredded cheddar cheese

Combine tomato sauce, kidney beans, onion and chili powder; pour over hamburger patties and simmer 15 minutes. Sprinkle burgers with cheese just before serving.

Italian Burgers Sauce
1 can (8 oz.) tomato sauce
¼ teaspoon oregano
¼ teaspoon basil
¼ cup water
Mozzarella cheese slices

Combine tomato sauce, oregano, basil and water; pour over hamburger patties and simmer 15 minutes. Top each burger with a slice of cheese just before serving.

Western Barbecue Burgers Sauce
1 can (8 oz.) tomato sauce
1 teaspoon Worcestershire sauce
¼ teaspoon salt
¼ cup water
½ teaspoon liquid smoke

Combine all ingredients; pour over hamburger patties and simmer 15 minutes. If desired, the sauce may be prepared and served over the cooked burgers.

Oven Pot Roast

Yield: 6 to 8 servings

3 to 3½ pounds chuck, round or rump
   roast
½ cup water
1 package (1¾ oz.) dry onion soup mix
2 medium carrots, cut into 1-inch pieces
2 medium potatoes, cut into quarters
1 cup celery, cut into ½ inch pieces
1 onion, wedged

Trim fat from meat. Place meat on large piece of heavy-duty aluminum foil in roasting pan. Mix water and dry onion soup mix. Pour over meat. Bring ends of foil over meat and seal in "drugstore" wrap. Roast. Temperature: 350°F. Time: 2 hours. Open foil carefully; add vegetables; cook additional 30 to 35 minutes or until vegetables are done.

Sloppy Joe

Yield: 8 servings

1 tablespoon salad oil
1 cup chopped onion
1 pound ground beef
1 (1½-ounce) package Sloppy Joe
   seasoning mix
1 8-oz. can tomato sauce
1 cup water
¼ cup chopped green pepper
4 hamburger buns, split
1 cup grated cheddar cheese

Sauté onion in hot oil for 1 minute. Brown beef. Add seasoning mix, tomato sauce, water and green pepper. Bring to a boil; cover and simmer 10 minutes. Uncover and simmer additional, 5 minutes. Serve on hamburger buns. Sprinkle with cheese before serving.

Creole Macaroni

2 pounds ground beef
1 tablespoons butter or margarine

1 package (8 oz.) elbow macaroni,
cooked
1 medium onion, chopped
3 cans (8 oz.) tomato sauce
1 can (12 oz.) whole kernel
corn
1 green pepper, chopped
1 clove garlic, minced
2 tablespoons chopped
parsley
2 teaspoons chili powder
1¼ teaspoons salt
1 teaspoon hot pepper
sauce
½ teaspoon sugar
½ teaspoon oregano leaves
¼ pound grated sharp
cheddar cheese

In a large pot, brown beef in butter; add rest of ingredients except cheese. Bring to boil. Pour into 9 x 13 greased baking pan. Sprinkle cheese and bake at 350°F until cheese melts.

2 pounds flank steak

Marinade:
½ cup soy sauce
¼ cup sesame oil
¼ cup sugar
1 teaspoon monosodium glutamate
  (MSG), optional
2 cloves garlic, minced
¼ teaspoon salt
¼ teaspoon black pepper
⅓ cup minced green onions
2 teaspoons sesame seeds, toasted and
  crushed

Remove tendon and trim steak. Pound and score beef. Cut into 3 x 4-inch pieces. Combine marinade ingredients and spread on steak pieces. Marinate 1 hour or longer. Broil to desired doneness.

Bul Kogi
Barbecued Beef

Yield: 4 to 6 servings

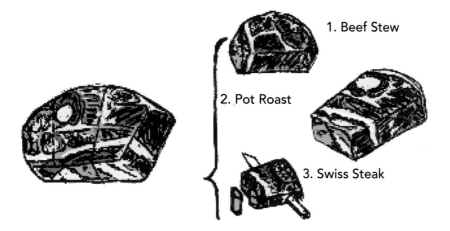

1. Beef Stew

2. Pot Roast

3. Swiss Steak

GUIDE TO BEEF CUTS

Labels on beef can be confusing since the name of the cut can vary from one market or region to the next. However, if you know where the "primal cuts" come from on a steer, you will be better able to decipher the supermarket labels, determine how tender and flavorful a steak might be and decide how to cook a particular cut.

The wholesalers divide the steer carcasses into nine sections which are referred to as the primal cuts (the tenderloin is part of the sirloin as shown on the illustration). The primal cuts are then broken down further into the retail cuts found at your market. The most tender steaks are from the cow's back—the rib, short loin and sirloin—because these muscles do less work. Steaks from the more heavily exercised chuck, plate and flank are tougher but have a good "beefy" flavor. When these less-tender cuts are cooked to medium rare or medium and thinly sliced across the grain, they're delicious and easier on your wallet. The toughest and leanest cuts are from the brisket, shank and round. They're best when slow cooking methods such as braising or roasting are used.

Loco Moco

Café 100 (Hilo, Island of Hawai'i)
Yield: 1 serving

The absolute mos' famous Big Island dish is probably loco moco. Loco moco is rice, hamburger, egg, and gravy. It's fairly easy to get the rice and egg right, although the hamburger and gravy may be a challenge for some. It started with teens from the Lincoln Wreckers Athletic Club who hung out at a restaurant called the Lincoln Grill, just across from Lincoln Park. Loco moco was originally sold for twenty-five cents to football players who requested a tasty, inexpensive, and filling dish.

Café 100 registered the loco moco name. When we think of loco moco today, we might think of Hilo's Café 100, which specializes in this dish. There are about twenty varieties of loco moco on sale, such as: bacon loco; chili loco; mahimahi loco; smoked sausage loco; stew loco; teriyaki loco; oyako loco; hot dog loco; and Spam® loco. If the special of the day is chicken chop suey, the special loco of the day may be chicken chop suey loco.

Café 100 was opened in 1946 by Richard Miyashiro, who named the restaurant to honor his fellow soldiers from the 100th Battalion. The tsunami of 1946 destroyed the restaurant only three months after it was opened. Richard rebuilt his dream restaurant in 1960. Twenty-seven days later it was destroyed in the 1960 tsunami. Café 100 re-opened in 1962 at its present location in Hilo.

Gravy stock:
2 pounds beef bones
1 carrot, diced
1 onion, diced
2 stalks celery, diced

Gravy:
¼ cup flour
¼ cup melted butter
1½ cups gravy stock, from stock pot
Salt and pepper to taste

Hamburger patties:
2 pounds lean ground beef
1½ teaspoons salt
¼ teaspoon black pepper
1 egg, beaten
½ cup chopped onion
¼ cup milk
½ cup bread crumbs

Loco moco (1 serving):
1 cup hot cooked rice
1 large fried hamburger patty
1 egg, cooked sunny side up
¼ cup brown gravy

Prepare gravy stock: Good gravy starts with a good stock. Put the diced carrots, onion, and celery in a baking pan. Place the beef bones on top and bake the pan in a 400°F oven for 45 minutes, until the bones are browned. Put the vegetables and bones in a large stock pot, add water to cover, and boil for 1 hour.

Prepare gravy: Whisk the flour into the melted butter over medium heat. Cook until flour and butter form a smooth paste; it should be hot enough to bubble a little. Slowly add the beef stock, stirring constantly so that no lumps form. Simmer for 10 minutes, or until the gravy begins to thicken. Season with salt and pepper to tastes.

Prepare hamburger patties: Combine all ingredients and form into patties.

To assemble loco moco: Place rice in a large bowl. Put a hamburger patty on top, add the cooked egg, and then pour gravy over the egg. Sound simple? As you see, it's not.

VARIATION:
Chili Moco: Top the hamburger patty with a serving of your favorite chili (before adding egg and gravy).

Bacon-Wrapped Meat loaf

Yield: 6 to 8 servings

Meat loaf is a comforting favorite for many families and it can be surprisingly different depending upon the creativity of the cook. A plate of piping hot meat loaf with gravy is hearty home cooking at its best!

1 cup fresh mushrooms, cleaned and
   minced
½ cup minced onion
¼ cup dry sherry
2 cloves garlic, minced
1½ teaspoons salt
½ teaspoon freshly ground pepper
1½ cups bread, torn into ½-inch pieces
¼ cup milk
1 large egg, beaten
1 pound lean ground beef
½ pound ground veal
½ pound ground pork
2 tablespoons light brown sugar
1 tablespoon Worcestershire sauce
8 slices center-cut bacon
Brown or mushroom gravy

In medium bowl, toss mushrooms with onion, sherry, garlic, salt and pepper; set aside. In a large mixing bowl, combine bread, milk and egg; stir well, lightly mashing bread until most of the liquid is absorbed. Add beef, veal, pork, brown sugar, Worcestershire and the onion-mushroom mixture. Using a large wooden spoon, gently mix just until all the ingredients are blended. Place meat mixture into a 9 x 13-inch baking pan. Shape the mixture into a rectangular loaf, about 10 x 4 inches. Wrap strips of bacon, crosswise, around the loaf, overlapping them slightly and tucking the ends securely under the loaf. Pat the loaf back into shape, if necessary. Meat loaf can be prepared up to this point 8 hours ahead and refrigerated until ready to bake. Bake. Temperature: 350°F. Time: 60 to 70 minutes or until an instant-read thermometer inserted into the center of the loaf reads 160°F. Remove from oven and broil meat loaf under broiler until bacon is brown and crisp, about 2 to 3 minutes. Let loaf rest 10 minutes before serving. Serve with brown or mushroom gravy of choice. In Hawai'i, ketchup is another favorite condiment for this dish.

TIP:
As a time-saver, bake meat loaf in muffin pans at 450°F for about 18 minutes.

Teri Meat loaf

Yield: 6 to 8 servings

This recipe fills me with nostalgia as my thoughts wander back to small kid times when this dish used to be served at get-togethers.

2 pounds ground beef
1 onion, minced
4 slices bread
½ cup milk
2 eggs
½ cup soy sauce
½ cup sugar
1 clove garlic, minced
1 tablespoon grated ginger
2 tablespoons mayonnaise

Combine ground beef and onions. Soak bread in milk; add eggs and milk mixture to meat. Mix soy sauce, sugar, garlic and ginger and add to meat. Add mayonnaise. Mix and shape into loaf. Place in loaf pan and bake at 350°F for about 45 to 60 minutes or until done.

Stuffed Cabbage

Yield: 4 to 6 servings

This dish was one of the more popular items offered at one of New York City's restaurants in the fifties.

12 large cabbage leaves, blanched
1 pound lean ground beef
1 teaspoon salt
¼ teaspoon pepper
¼ cup bread crumbs
½ cup minced onion
2 cans (8 oz. each) tomato sauce
¼ cup brown sugar, packed
¼ cup vinegar or lemon juice

Combine beef, salt, pepper, bread crumbs, onion and 1 can tomato sauce; mix well. Place equal portions of meat mixture in center of each cabbage leaf. Fold ends over, roll up and fasten with toothpicks.

Mix remaining ingredients and pour over cabbage rolls. Cover and cook over low heat for 30 minutes, basting occasionally. Uncover and cook additional 15 to 20 minutes.

Homemade Chili

Yield: 4 to 6 servings

A comforting dish, especially when served over fresh steamed rice with condiments of grated cheese and chopped onions.

1 pound lean ground beef
1 clove garlic, minced
¼ cup minced onion
¼ cup chopped green pepper
2 cans (8 oz. each) tomato sauce
1 teaspoon salt
½ teaspoon sugar
1 tablespoon chili powder
1 can (15½ oz.) red or kidney beans, undrained

Sauté beef, garlic, onion and green pepper. Add remaining ingredients and stir. Simmer, stirring occasionally, until chili is of desired thickness, about 30 minutes.

VARIATION:
Ground chicken or turkey may be substituted for beef.

Kahl Bi

Barbecued Shortribs

Yield: 4 to 6 servings

3 pounds thick shortribs

Marinade (see recipe on the right)

Butterfly shortribs by cutting parallel to the bone to within ¼-inch of opposite side; open to lay flat. Score meat on both sides. Combine marinade ingredients; mix well and marinate meat 4 hours or longer. Broil to desired doneness.

TIP:
Marinate meat and poultry in a large zipper-top plastic bag. Place the marinade directly into the bag, close it and shake to mix. Add meat, press out excess air and reseal. Place in the refrigerator and turn bag occasionally.

Teriyaki Beef

Yield: 4 to 6 servings

Teriyaki sauce adds a wonderful flavor to any meat, especially these thin slices of beef.

1 pound beef, sliced thinly

<u>Marinade:</u>
½ cup brown sugar, packed
½ cup soy sauce
¼ cup sake (rice wine) or sherry
¼ teaspoon monosodium glutamate (MSG), optional
1 clove garlic, crushed
1½-inch slice ginger root, crushed or ¼ teaspoon powdered ginger

Combine marinade ingredients and marinate beef 15 to 20 minutes. Broil, turning once and basting occasionally until of desired doneness, about 3 to 4 minutes. Serve hot.

How to make a rib roast do double duty:

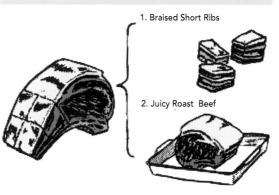

1. Braised Short Ribs

2. Juicy Roast Beef

PORK

Pork is considered the other white meat and it is not what it used to be. Today's pork has changed from "fatty" to lean. To get the most in flavor and tenderness for today's pork, cooking times and internal temperatures have changed so please refer to an updated detailed pork cooking information chart for specifics.

Adobo

Filipino-Style Pickled Pork

Yield: 3 to 4 servings

Adobo is basic Filipino comfort food that can be found in hundreds of variations. It comes from a long tradition of meat dishes with a vinegar base, also found in the cuisines of Spain and France. Vinegar gives adobo its tang, but when correctly made, the dish should be a good balance of flavors.

2 pounds fresh pork butt, medium cubed
1 teaspoon garlic salt
½ teaspoon ground black pepper
½ cup soy sauce
1 tablespoon fresh minced garlic
⅓ cup cider vinegar
4 bay leaves, crumbled

Combine all ingredients; mix well and marinate pork overnight in refrigerator. Place everything in a skillet; cover and cook over medium heat, stirring occasionally, until pork is browned and tender, about 30 to 45 minutes. Meat will be crispy on outside and all liquid in pan will have been absorbed. Serve very hot; may be reheated the next day.

VARIATION:
Chicken Adobo: Substitute 3 pounds chicken, cut into serving pieces, for pork; add 1 tablespoon grated ginger to sauce mixture.

Roast Pork Loin

Yield: 4 to 6 servings

Roasted pork loin makes an excellent entrée for that special occasion. Transform the leftovers into other meals during the week.

4-pound boneless pork loin roast, trimmed

Brine:
8 cups cold apple cider or juice
¾ cup kosher salt
¼ cup light brown sugar
1 clove garlic, smashed
2 sprigs fresh thyme

For the roast:
¼ cup maple syrup
3 tablespoons Dijon mustard
1 teaspoon chopped fresh thyme
½ teaspoon fresh ground pepper; more to taste

Brine the pork: Combine 2 cups of the apple cider or juice with the salt, brown sugar, garlic and thyme in a 3-quart saucepan; bring to a boil over high heat, stirring to dissolve salt and sugar, about 3 to 4 minutes. Add the remaining apple cider or juice and cool to room temperature. Transfer to a large container; add the pork. Cover and refrigerate overnight.

Roast the pork: Place rack in center position of oven; heat oven to 450°F. In a small bowl, mix together maple syrup, mustard, thyme and pepper. Drain the pork and pat dry with paper towels; brush mustard mixture all over pork. Place pork, fat side up, in roasting pan. Roast until pork just begins to brown, about 15 minutes. Reduce heat to 350°F and continue roasting 30 to 50 minutes more or until thermometer inserted in thickest part of the loin registers 145°F. Let rest 10 minutes then cut about one-third of pork into thin slices. Top with juices to serve.

Allow remaining pork to cool to room temperature, wrap well with foil and refrigerate for up to 5 days before using in other recipes.

Use leftover Roast Pork:

- Sandwiches: Make grilled roast pork sandwiches.
- Lettuce cups: Cut leftover pork into matchstick pieces; sauté in oil 1 minute. Season with salt, pepper and oyster sauce to taste. Add ½ cup chopped green onion and dried shiitake mushrooms, stemmed and minced. Serve in iceberg lettuce cups.
- Stews: Prepare shellfish stew with mussels, clams and shrimp. Toss in pork as a meaty counterpart.
- Pasta: Brown pieces of pork and toss with cabbage, Parmesan cheese and cooked penne.
- Salads: Cut pork into strips and sprinkle over salad greens.
- Cobb Salad: Dice pork and sprinkle across romaine with avocado, corn and tomatoes.

Barbecued Cantonese Ribs

Yield: 4 to 6 servings

Yummy! This is finger-lickin' good!

3 pounds pork loin back ribs

Marinade:
½ cup soy sauce
½ cup brown sugar, packed
½ cup tomato ketchup
1 tablespoon sherry
1 teaspoon ginger juice
1 clove garlic, crushed
Dash of monosodium glutamate (MSG), optional

Combine ingredients for marinade. Marinate ribs for 3 hours. Place on a rack in a shallow roasting pan. Roast at 350°F for 30 minutes on one side; turn and roast for an additional 30 minutes or until done. Cut ribs apart into 1½-inch pieces to serve.

How to make 3 meals from one pork butt/shoulder roast:

1. Pork Roast
2. Pork Steaks
3. Pork Chop Suey

Pork Tofu

Yield: 4 to 6 servings

Enjoy this nutritious, light, and tasty dish!

½ pound pork, sliced thin
1½ tablespoons salad oil
2½ tablespoons sugar
⅓ cup soy sauce
2 thin slices fresh ginger root, crushed
½ teaspoon sake (rice wine)
1 medium carrot, cut into thin strips
3 stalks green onion, cut into 1-inch
  lengths
1 small round onion, sliced thin
1 block tofu (bean curd), cut into 1-inch
  cubes, drained

Stir-fry pork in hot oil. Add sugar, soy sauce, ginger root and sake. Bring to boil. Add carrot, green onion and round onion; cook over low heat 3 minutes. Add tofu and cook additional 4 minutes. Serve hot with steamed rice.

> **TIP:**
> To soften brown sugar, put it into a jar with a tight-fitting cover. Place a very damp cloth in a dish on the sugar in the jar. Moisten the cloth often until sugar is soft.

Baked Hoisin Barbecue Ribs

Yield: 6 to 8 servings

These pork ribs are flavored with hoisin—a spicy, salty-sweet brown sauce made of soybeans, sugar, garlic, Chinese five-spice powder, chili and red rice for coloring—and are then glazed with a layer of delicious honey.

2 racks of pork ribs
1 jar (15 oz.) hoisin sauce
1 jar (12 oz.) honey

Remove excess fat and tissues from ribs. Brush hoisin sauce on both sides and let stand in refrigerator overnight. Place pork ribs on rack on foil-lined baking pans. Brush with additional hoisin sauce on one side.

Bake at 350°F for 30 minutes; turn, brush with sauce on other side and bake additional 30 minutes or until done. Brush honey on both sides and leave in oven additional 5 minutes to glaze. Remove from oven, let stand 5 minutes before separating ribs. Cut into desired sizes to serve.

Char Siu

Yield: about 2 pounds

An all-time favorite—char siu is versatile and served as an entreé, side dish, or pūpū. It is also often served as a garnish for a variety of dishes.

2 pounds lean pork

Seasoning:
2 tablespoons soy sauce
1 teaspoon salt
¼ cup sugar
½ teaspoon Chinese Five Spices
¼ cup red bean curd
2 tablespoons sherry
½ teaspoon red food coloring

Cut pork into 1 x 2 x 6-inch strips. Combine Seasoning ingredients and marinate pork for at least one hour. Place on rack in shallow roasting pan lined with foil and roast. Temperature: 375°F. Time: 1 hour. Slice thinly and serve warm or cold as a side dish or garnish.

Haole Laulau

Yield: 8 servings

This is an easier version of the traditional laulau. Try it; you'll like it.

2 ounces salted butterfish, optional
3 packages (10 oz. each) fresh frozen leaf spinach or 2 pounds fresh spinach, washed and drained
3 to 4 pounds pork butt, cut into 2-inch cubes
2 teaspoons salt
¼ teaspoon fresh ground pepper

Soak butterfish in clear water for an hour; drain and slice. Layer spinach, pork and butterfish in a greased casserole dish. Season with salt and pepper. Cover casserole and bake. Temperature: 350°F. Time: 1 hour or until done.

Oven Kālua Pork

Yield: 8 to 10 servings

Oven kālua pork needs very little attention while it is roasting. It is delicious as a sandwich filling, an entrée or even as a garnish to salads.

4 pounds pork butt
¼ cup liquid smoke
2 tablespoons rock salt
4 large ti leaves, rib removed

Score pork on all sides, making ¼-inch deep slits 1 inch apart. Rub salt into slits, then rub all sides with liquid smoke. Wrap in leaves, then in aluminum foil and seal. Let stand 30 to 45 minutes. Place on rack in shallow roasting pan. Roast. Temperature: 550°F for 45 minutes, then at 400°F for 3½ hours or until done. Shred cooked pork and let stand in light brine solution before serving.

Baked Pork 'N Beans

Yield: 4 to 6 servings

Back in the day, this comfort food was often served at our schools. It was specifically delicious when served with lots of bacon bits.

1 (1-pound 15-ounce) can pork and beans
⅓ cup tomato ketchup
¼ cup minced onion
1 teaspoon dry mustard
⅓ cup brown sugar, packed
2 slices bacon, diced
4 frankfurters, sliced

Combine all ingredients in a greased 1½-quart casserole. Bake. Temperature: 350°F. Time: 1 hour.

Carne De Vinha D'Alhos

Pickled Pot Roast

Yield: 4 to 6 servings

This dish is one of the comfort foods for the Portuguese. The tart vinegar flavored pork dish is unique and delicious.

3 to 4 pounds pork butt or shoulder roast

Marinade:
1¼ cups cider vinegar
1 tablespoon salt
1 teaspoons chopped red pepper
3 cloves garlic, minced
2 bay leaves
5 whole cloves
⅛ teaspoon sage
¼ teaspoon powdered thyme

Combine Marinade ingredients and marinate pork in refrigerator for 3 to 5 days, turning daily to flavor evenly.

Place pork and marinade in baking dish; cover and bake at 375°F for 2½ hours or until done. If desired, remove cover during last 15 minutes to brown roast.

Baked Spareribs

Yield: 4 to 6 servings

What's not to like about succulent ribs seasoned with the exotic Chinese five-spice powder, nam yoy, honey, sherry and garlic.

2½ pounds pork spareribs

Marinade:
2 teaspoons Chinese five-spice powder
4 teaspoons salt
¼ cup red bean curd (nam yoy)
2 tablespoons honey
2 teaspoons sherry
1 clove garlic, crushed
Few drops red food coloring

Cut spareribs into 1 x 3-inch pieces. Combine marinade ingredients. Brush half of marinade over both sides of spareribs. Marinate about 30 minutes. Reserve other half of marinade to baste ribs last 30 minutes of baking.

Place ribs on rack in shallow roasting pan. Bake. Temperature: 350°F. Time: 1 hour.

Sweet-Sour Spareribs

Yield: 6 to 8 servings

Like Asian food? You'll love this easy recipe.

3 pounds spareribs, cut into 2-inch pieces

Marinade:
3 tablespoons sherry
5 tablespoons soy sauce
¾ cup cornstarch

½ cup salad oil for frying

Sweet-Sour Sauce:
2 tablespoons cornstarch
¾ cup brown sugar, packed
¾ cup cider vinegar
¾ cup pineapple juice
¼ cup soy sauce

2 round onions, wedged
2 cups pineapple chunks
1 green pepper, wedged

Mix together all ingredients for marinade. Marinate spareribs in marinade 30 minutes. Slowly brown spareribs in salad oil heated to 350°F. Cover and simmer 25 minutes.

Combine Sweet-Sour Sauce ingredients and add to the pork. Cover and simmer additional 25 to 30 minutes, stirring occasionally.

Add onions, pineapple and green pepper. Cover and simmer until vegetables are tender, about 3 minutes.

How to get 3 fresh-cooked meals from a pork loin roast:

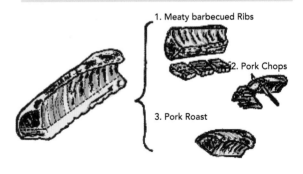

1. Meaty barbecued Ribs

2. Pork Chops

3. Pork Roast

Crispy Roast Pork

Yield: 6 servings

Succulent slabs of freshly roasted pork with its crispy skin can be found hanging on display in Chinatown's open markets.

2 pounds belly pork

Marinade:
3 tablespoons soy sauce
5 tablespoons hoisin sauce
2 tablespoons sherry
2 tablespoons sugar
¼ teaspoon Chinese Five Spices
¼ teaspoon monosodium glutamate (MSG), optional
1½-inch slice ginger, crushed

Lightly score pork on meaty side. Combine marinade ingredients and rub on meaty side (do not get any sauce on skin). Let stand for 15 minutes. Place pork on rack, skin side up. Bake at 425°F for 15 minutes, then 375°F for 40 to 50 minutes, or until skin is blistered. Slice and serve with oyster sauce.

Rafute

Okinawan Pot Roast Pork

Yield: 6 to 8 servings

Rafute is my favorite Okinawan dish. The braised pork slices are served without the liquid and the sauce is saved and used as the basis for other dishes.

4 to 5 pounds lean pork butt

Sauce:
2 cups soy sauce
½ cup water
2½ cups sugar
½ cup mirin (sweet rice wine) or cooking wine, optional
1 piece (1-inch) ginger, crushed
1 to 2 cloves garlic, crushed (optional)

Combine sauce ingredients in a large saucepan; mix well and marinate pork overnight in the refrigerator. Cover and cook over high heat until sauce comes to a boil. Lower heat and continue cooking, turning meat over occasionally, for 3 to 4 hours or until meat is tender. Add more sauce, if necessary.

TIP:
Chill the sauce to solidify and remove the fat before serving.

POULTRY

Poultry, especially chicken, continues to gain in popularity because most people like it for it's economical and relatively low in fat. It was brought to America in the 1700s and were considered a delicacy at that time. Chicken has always been important to us for the eggs they lay to its versatility in the creation of numerous delicious dishes.

HOW TO BONE CHICKEN BREASTS:

1. Place skin-side down. With knife, cut through white gristle at neck end; bend back and press flat to expose heel bone.
2. Loosen heel bone with finger. Insert knife tip and work knife under bone to cut meat away from bone. Work from ends of wishbone; scrape flesh away from each piece of bone.

Cold Chicken with Ginger Sauce

Yield: 6 servings

2 quarts water
1 tablespoon salt
1 small piece ginger root, crushed
4 pounds roasting chicken
¾ cup salad oil
½ teaspoon salt
1 clove garlic, minced
⅓ cup minced ginger root
⅓ cup minced green onions
1 tablespoon chopped Chinese parsley

In a sauce pot, bring water, the 1 tablespoon salt, and ginger to a boil. Add whole chicken, cover, and immediately turn lo lowest heat; cook for 45 minutes or until done. Remove chicken from broth and rinse quickly with cold water; drain. Freeze broth for later use. Cut chicken into bite-size pieces; arrange on serving dish. Heal oil with the ½ teaspoon salt; cool. Stir in garlic, minced ginger, and green onions. Pour sauce over chicken and garnish with parsley to serve.

Chinese-Style Roast Duck

Yield: 6 to 8 servings

The honey glazed duck is the perfect fare for any family dinner. It is simply ravished.

4 to 5-pound duck

Seasoning:
1 teaspoon Chinese five-spice powder
½ teaspoon pepper
1 teaspoon sugar
½ teaspoon salt
1 tablespoon sherry

Glaze:
1 tablespoon honey
½ cup boiling water

Clean duck and wipe dry. Combine seasoning ingredients and brush cavity until well-coated. Combine honey and water; pour over duck.

Place duck on a rack in a shallow pan. Roast. Temperature: 325°F. Time: 2 to 2½ hours or until done.

Lemon Chicken

Yield: 4 to 6 servings

1 fryer chicken

Marinade:
½ teaspoon salt
1 tablespoon sherry
1 tablespoon soy sauce

2 eggs, beaten
¼ cup cornstarch
½ teaspoon baking powder
2 cups salad oil for frying

Lemon Sauce:
1 tablespoon salad oil
1 teaspoon salt
3 tablespoons sugar
1 tablespoon cornstarch
1 to 2 tablespoons lemon juice
1 cup canned chicken broth

1 to 2 lemons, sliced thin for garnish

Cut chicken into bite-sized pieces. Marinate chicken in salt, sherry and soy sauce for 15 minutes.

Combine eggs, cornstarch and baking powder. Beat to form a smooth batter. Heat oil to 365°F. Coat chicken pieces with batter and deep-fry for 4 to 5 minutes or until well-browned. Drain on absorbent paper.

To prepare Lemon Sauce, heat oil and slowly add remaining sauce ingredients. Stir constantly until sauce is clear. Pour Lemon Sauce over chicken to serve. Garnish with lemon slices.

VARIATION:
Orange Chicken: Substitute orange juice for lemon juice.

Teriyaki Chicken

Yield: 4 to 6 servings

This is probably one of the most requested main dish Islanders ask for when ordering plate lunch.

3 to 4 pounds fryer chicken pieces
¼ cup salad oil
1½ inch slice fresh ginger root, crushed
2 cloves garlic, crushed
1 tablespoon sherry
½ cup soy sauce
½ cup water
⅓ cup brown sugar, packed

Heat oil, ginger and garlic in skillet. Fry chicken until light brown. Add remaining ingredients. Cover and cook slowly over medium-low heat for 45 minutes or until done.

Minute Chicken

Yield: 6 servings

Boneless chicken pieces flavor this easy stir-fry dish ever so quickly. It's a winner served over hot steamed rice!

3 pounds boneless chicken pieces
3 tablespoons flour
¼ cup salad oil
2 cloves garlic, crushed
¾ cup chopped green onions
⅓ cup chopped Chinese parsley
1 tablespoon sugar
⅓ cup oyster sauce
⅓ cup water
¼ teaspoon pepper

Garnish:
Chinese parsley

Cut chicken info bite-sized pieces. Coat with flour; let stand for 10 minutes. In wok or skillet, heat oil and garlic until oil is sizzling. Add chicken and stir-fry until browned. Add remaining ingredients; cook additional 1 to 2 minutes. Garnish with additional Chinese parsley.

Mochiko Chicken

Serves 4 to 6

The crispy, savory pieces of chicken are among one of Hawai`i's favorites.

2 pounds boneless chicken thighs
¼ cup mochiko
¼ cup cornstarch
¼ cup sugar
5 tablespoons soy sauce
¼ cup minced green onions
2 eggs, beaten
2 cloves garlic, minced
½ teaspoon salt

In large bowl, mix together all ingredients, except chicken. Add chicken and marinate in mixture for 2 to 12 hours. Deep-fry or pan-fry chicken in hot oil until browned on both sides and cooked. Drain on absorbent paper, cut into serving pieces and serve hot or at room temperature.

Yakitori
Chicken Kabobs

Yield: About 16 kabobs

Whenever we had a cook-out, Yakitori was certain to be on the menu. The marinade can also be used for pork and beef kabobs.

1 pound boneless, skinless chicken, cubed
Bamboo skewers

Marinade:
⅓ cup soy sauce
¼ cup sugar
1 clove garlic, crushed
1 small piece ginger root, crushed

Thread 3 pieces of chicken on each skewer. Combine marinade ingredients; marinate chicken for 30 minutes. Place skewers on the rack of a broiler pan and broil for about 5 minutes on one side; turn and broil an additional 3 minutes or until done.

Southern Fried Chicken

Yield: 4 servings

1 2 to 2½ pound broiler fryer chicken,
   cut in serving pieces
½ cup flour
1 teaspoon salt
1 teaspoon paprika
Dash of pepper
2 cups canola oil for frying

Mix flour, salt, paprika and pepper, in plastic or paper bag. Add chicken pieces, a few pieces at a time, and shake until, well-coated. Heat oil, in skillet. Add chicken, skin side down. Cook uncovered, for 10 to 15 minutes on each side or until done. Drain on absorbent paper.

Mix-and-Match Chicken Bake

Yield: 4 to 6 servings

3 cups cooked rice
2 jars (5½ oz. each) chicken, cut
¼ cup minced onion
⅓ cup sliced stuffed olives
1 cup cooked peas
1 can (10½ oz.) condensed cream of
** chicken soup**
½ cup milk
¾ cup grated, processed American
** cheese**
1 cup crushed potato chips

Combine rice, chicken, onion, olives and peas. Combine soup, milk and cheese and mix; add to rice mixture and mix gently. Place in greased 1-quart casserole. Top with potato chips. Bake. Temperature: 400°F. Time: 30 to 35 minutes.

HOW TO CUT UP A WHOLE CHICKEN

1. Cut legs off by cutting skin between thighs and body.
2. Lift and bend chicken legs back until hip joints are loose.
3. Remove leg fom body.
4. Separate thigh and drumstick.
5. Remove wing from body by cutting on inside of wing just over the joint.
6. Cut body into breast and back sections.
7. Cut breast, with skin-side down, through white cartilage at "V" of neck.
8. Cut breast in half lengthwise.

VARIATIONS: Use the following combinations.

CEREAL PRODUCT	MEAT	VEGETABLE	SOUP	TOPPING
3 cups cooked macaroni	2 cans (7 oz. each) tuna, rinsed and	1 cup cooked green beans or peas drained	1 can (10 ½ oz.) condensed cream of mushroom soup	1 cup chow mein noodles
3 cups cooked noodles	2 cups cubed cooked ham	1 cup cooked corn or peas	1 can (10 oz.) condensed cream of celery soup	1 cup crushed corn chips
3 cups cooked rice	2 cans (4½ oz. each) shrimp, rinsed and drained	1 cup cooked peas	1 can (10½ oz.) frozen cream of shrimp soup	1 cup toasted slivered almonds

Turkey/Chicken ala King

Yield: 4 to 6 servings

¼ cup butter or margarine
¼ cup flour
½ teaspoon salt
Dash white pepper
1 cup chicken stock
1 cup evaporated milk
1 (10-ounce) package frozen peas and carrots, thawed and drained, optional
3 to 4 cups cooked chicken, diced

Melt butter or margarine in skillet; blend in flour, salt, and pepper. Slowly add chicken stock, evaporated milk, peas and carrots, and chicken; cook 4 to 5 minutes or until thickened. Serve hot over hot steamed rice or mashed potatoes.

Oven Baked Chicken

Yield: 4 servings

8 chicken thighs (about 3 pounds), skin removed
½ teaspoon salt
Pepper, to taste
3 tablespoons grated parmesan cheese
½ cup mayonnaise
4 cups cornflakes, crushed

Preheat oven to 375°F. Sprinkle chicken on both sides with salt, pepper and cheese. Coat with mayonnaise, then roll in cornflakes. Bake for 45 minutes or until juices run clear.

Chicken Sukiyaki

Yield: 4 to 6 servings

The ever-popular sukiyaki originated in ancient days when farmers or hunters in Japan often killed animals and cooked their meat over an open fire on available utensils, such as a plow. Therefore, "sukiyaki" literally means "broiled on the blade of a plow."

1½ pounds boneless chicken, cut into bite-sized pieces
1 tablespoon butter or margarine
½ cup chicken broth
¼ cup sugar
¼ cup soy sauce
2 tablespoons sake (Japanese rice wine)
1 cup bamboo shoots, sliced
1 cup mushrooms (matsutake), sliced
1 cup shirataki (yam flour noodles)
1 onion, sliced
1½ cups green onion, cut into 1½ inch lengths
4 cups watercress, cut into 2-inch lengths

Sauté chicken in butter or margarine. Add chicken stock, sugar, soy sauce and sake; cook for 2 minutes over medium heat. Add bamboo shoots, mushrooms and shirataki; cook additional 2 minutes.

Add sliced onion, green onion and watercress. Cook over medium heat only until vegetables are cooked.

TIP:
1 can (15 oz.) "Sukiyaki-no-tomo" may be substituted for bamboo shoots, mushrooms, and shirataki.

Chicken Cacciatore

Yield: 4 to 6 servings

3-pound fryer chicken, cut into serving
  pieces
½ cup flour
½ teaspoon salt
¼ teaspoon pepper
⅓ cup salad oil
2 medium onions, sliced
3 cloves garlic, minced
1 can (1 pound) whole tomatoes
1 can (8 oz.) tomato sauce
1 teaspoon salt
1 ½ teaspoons oregano
½ teaspoon basil
½ teaspoon celery seed
¼ teaspoon pepper
¼ cup sherry

Dredge chicken in flour, salt and pepper mixture. Brown chicken in salad oil. Remove chicken from pan and sauté onions and garlic. Return chicken to skillet and add all remaining ingredients, except Sautérne. Cover and simmer over medium heat for 40 minutes. Stir in Sautérne and simmer, uncovered, for 20 minutes longer. Serve over cooked spaghetti or steamed rice.

Wikiwiki Turkey Bake

Yield: 6 to 8 servings

Here's a quick 'n easy casserole dish that can be ready to serve in 30 minutes. Economical too!

2 cups cooked turkey
1 cup nuts
2 cups button mushrooms, drained
1 can (6 oz.) tiny round onions, drained
2 cans cream of mushroom soup
⅓ cup sherry

Topping:
1 cup fine bread crumbs
¼ cup melted butter or margarine

Cut turkey into bite-sized pieces, combine with nuts, mushrooms and onions. Place in 1½ quart casserole. Mix together mushroom soup and wine. Pour over turkey mixture and blend.

Prepare topping by mixing bread crumbs and melted butter or margarine. Sprinkle over top of casserole. Bake. Temperature: 350°F. Time: 15 minutes.

Oven Kālua Turkey

Yield: 8 to 10 servings

12 pounds turkey
12 ti leaves
1 banana leaf
½ cup butter or margarine, softened
3 tablespoons Hawaiian salt
2 teaspoons liquid smoke

Rinse and drain turkey. Line a large baking pan with foil. Wash ti leaves and banana leaf; remove fibrous parts of the veins. Line baking pan with ti leaves radiating from center; place half of the banana leaf in bottom of pan. Place turkey on leaves. Rub remaining ingredients on inside and outside of turkey. Place remaining half of banana leaf over turkey; fold leaves around turkey. Crimp foil around turkey and cover pan tightly with additional foil. Roast in electric oven at 375°F for 6 hours. Shred turkey, adding enough of the pan liquid to moisten meat.

Chicken Pot Pie

Yield: about 4 servings

With the use of rotisserie cooked chicken, frozen and canned products, here is an easy version of Chicken Pot Pie which can be ready in less than an hour.

2 tablespoons butter or margarine
¼ cup chopped celery
¼ cup chopped onion
1 refrigerated pie crust, softened to room temperature
1 can (10½ oz.) condensed cream of chicken soup
1 cup milk
¼ teaspoon salt
Freshly ground pepper to taste
2 cups cubed cooked chicken breast
1 bag (1 pound) frozen mixed vegetables

Melt butter or margarine in 3-quart saucepan; add celery and onion and cook over medium heat until tender. Stir in soup, milk, salt and pepper. Cook until thoroughly heated. Stir in chicken and thawed vegetables; pour into ungreased 2-quart casserole or 10-inch quiche pan. Place crust over chicken mixture. Roll up edges of crust to fit top of casserole; flute edges. Cut slits in 3 places in crust. Bake. Temperature: 400°F. Time: 40 to 50 minutes or until golden brown. Let stand 10 minutes before serving.

VARIATION:
Turkey Pot Pie: Substitute turkey for chicken.

SEAFOOD

Fish is gaining popularity as a light entrée, one that is extremely healthful as it is full of protein and light on fat. Furthermore, it is versatile and easy to prepare, which fits right into today's fast-paced lifestyle.

Asian-Style Steamed Fish

Yield: 2 to 4 servings

Cooks and diners alike focus on flavor and freshness today. This delicious dish is a case in point.

1 mullet, kūmū or catfish, scaled and cleaned
½ teaspoon salt
4 slices round onion
¼ cup bamboo shoots, slivered
½ cup green onion, cut in 1-inch lengths
5 slices lemon
2 shiitake mushrooms, softened in water and slivered

Sauce:
¼ teaspoon grated fresh ginger root
2 tablespoons soy sauce

Salt fish; place on heat resistant platter and arrange round onion, bamboo shoots, green onion, lemon and mushrooms on fish. Cover and steam 20 to 25 minutes or until done. Serve with ginger-soy sauce.

Baked Teri Salmon

Yield: 4 servings

Salmon is not often served with a teriyaki sauce but the Asian flavor to this dish is very appealing. It is especially good when served as a topping to a crisp, green garden salad or as an entrée accompanied by cooked green beans and steamed rice.

4 salmon steaks

Sauce:
½ cup soy sauce
⅓ cup sugar
¼ cup mirin (sweet rice wine)
1 tablespoon grated fresh ginger
1 clove garlic, mashed
2 tablespoons sesame oil
¼ cup salad oil

Garnish:
Chopped green onion

Pan-broil salmon steaks in hot non-stick skillet until lightly brown on both sides. Combine all sauce ingredients; stir to combine and pour over salmon steaks. Bring sauce to a simmer over medium heat. Garnish with green onions and serve immediately with cooked green vegetables and steamed rice.

Fishburger

Yield: 4 to 6 servings

1 pound filet of fish, finely chopped
1 small round onion, minced
¼ cup chopped green onion
3 slices stale bread, cut in ¼-inch cubes
1 egg, beaten
½ teaspoon salt
Dash of pepper

Combine all ingredients and mix thoroughly. Form into 3-inch patties. Pan fry in hot oil until golden. Serve with soy sauce or tartar sauce.

Creamed Tuna

Yield: 4 to 6 servings

¼ cup margarine or butter
¼ cup flour
½ teaspoon salt
¼ teaspoon white pepper
2 cups milk
2 6½-ounce cans tuna, drained
1 8½-ounce can peas and carrots, drained

Melt butter, blend in flour, salt, and pepper. Add milk gradually, stirring constantly; cook over low heat until thickened. Add tuna, peas and carrots; heat through. Serve over steamed rice or mashed potatoes.

Hawaiian Shrimp Curry

Yield: about 6 servings

Many of Hawai'i's hostesses love to serve this curry when entertaining because the presentation is usually colorful and beautiful...besides, it is simp-ly onolicious!

¼ cup butter or margarine
1 small onion, minced
1 clove garlic, minced
1 small piece ginger root, minced
1½ tablespoons curry powder
⅓ cup flour
1½ teaspoons salt
1 can (12 oz.) frozen coconut milk, thawed
1¼ cups chicken broth
1¾ pounds medium shrimp, shelled and cleaned

Suggested condiments:
Chutney
Minced green onion
Chopped hard-cooked eggs
Chopped macadamia nuts
Shredded coconut
Chopped raisins
Crisp crumbled bacon

Melt butter or margarine in saucepan and sauté onion, garlic and ginger until tender. Add curry powder, flour and salt; slowly stir in coconut milk and broth. Cover over medium heat, stirring constantly, until mixture thickens. Stir in shrimp; cook until shrimp turns pink and heated through. Serve over hot steamed rice with condiments of choice.

VARIATION:
Hawaiian Chicken Curry: Substitute cooked chicken for shrimp.

Fried 'Ahi or Aku

Yield: 4 servings

Here's a new twist to simple fried fish that makes this dish a "winner."

1 pound 'ahi or aku belly filet (skin on)
½ cup flour
1 teaspoon garlic salt
¼ teaspoon cayenne
¼ teaspoon Cajun spices
1 quart canola oil for frying

Cut fish into serving slices; pat dry and dredge in mixture of flour, garlic, salt, cayenne and Cajun spices on both sides.

Heat oil in skillet and cook fish in hot oil until golden brown and crispy on both sides. Drain on absorbent paper and serve immediately. Serve with soy or tartar sauce.

Seafood Tempura

Yield: Varies

Tempura ranks among the great dishes of Hawai'i, if not the world, and is known throughout for its unmatched delicacy. Tempura was introduced centuries ago to Japan by the Portuguese and Spanish who established missions in southern Japan. It is a food dipped in batter then deep fried and served with a dipping sauce mixed with grated daikon. If you prefer a lighter batter, use #2.

Batter #1 (Yields 1¾ cups):
½ cup flour
½ cup cornstarch
½ cup ice-cold water
1 egg, beaten

Batter #2 (Yields 2¼ cups):
⅔ cup cake flour
⅓ cup cornstarch
1 cup ice-cold water
1 egg, beaten

Sift together dry ingredients; set aside. In a separate bowl add water to egg; stir well. Add dry ingredients all at once to egg-water mixture; stir briefly, just enough to combine mixture. The batter will be lumpy. Do not overmix. Heat oil to 365 to 375°F. Dip cleaned and prepared seafood or vegetables into batter and deep fry in oil until lightly browned. Drain on absorbant paper and serve with tempura sauce while hot.

Suggested tempura ingredients:
- Seafoods: Fish fillet (mahi, 'ahi, sole, sea bass, etc.), shrimp (shelled and cleaned with tails on), calamari, etc.
- Vegetables: Asparagus spears, burdock root, lotus root, bamboo shoots, ginko nuts on skewers, sweet potato slices, carrot slices, green beans, bell pepper slices, sweet onion slices, broccoli crowns, cauliflower, zucchini slices, mushrooms, shiso (beefsteak plant leaves), parsley, nori (laver), pumpkin slices, okra, eggplant, etc.

Tempura Sauce #1 (Yields 1½ cups):
1 cup water
½ teaspoon dashi-no-moto
¼ cup mirin (sweet rice wine)
¼ cup soy sauce
1 tablespoon sugar

Combine all ingredients and bring to a boil. Cool. Add condiments to serve.

Tempura Sauce #2 (Yields 2 cups):
1 piece (5-inch) dashi konbu
2 cups boiling water
½ cup dried bonito flakes
2 teaspoons soy sauce
½ teaspoon salt
½ teaspoon sugar

Condiments for Sauce:
½ cup grated daikon (white radish)
1 tablespoon minced green onion

Add konbu to boiling water; cook 10 minutes. Add bonito flakes; cook 3 minutes; strain. Add remaining ingredients and bring to a boil. Cool. Add condiments to serve.

TIPS FOR GREAT TEMPURA:

- Use ice-cold water
- Keep batter chilled
- Do not overmix batter; leave lumps
- Coat food lightly with batter
- Prepare small quantity of batter at a time
- Cook small quantities at a time
- Serve hot

Misoyaki Butterfish

Yield: About 3 to 4 servings

Misoyaki Butterfish is a traditional Japanese dish which is often featured on teishoku trays as well as an entreé served on fine china in upscale restaurants.

1½ pounds butterfish fillet steaks

Miso Sauce:
1½ cups miso
¾ cup sugar
1 to 2 tablespoons mirin
½ teaspoon grated fresh ginger root

Combine Miso Sauce ingredients; mix well to blend ingredients. Marinate fish in Miso Sauce overnight or up to 2 to 3 days; shake off excess marinade before cooking. If whole fish is used, cut slashes on each side of fish and salt lightly. Stuff fish cavity with Miso Sauce; fry or broil.

Broil fish in oven broiler or on outdoor grill over medium to high heat for 3 to 5 minutes on each side or until of desired doneness.

Crusted Curried Mahimahi

Yield: about 4 servings

This dish was created for a group of visitors from California about 45 years ago and it is still one of my favorite party dishes.

1 pound mahimahi fillet
1 egg, slightly beaten
1 cup cornflake crumbs or panko
1 quart salad oil for frying

Marinade:
1 tablespoon sugar
1 teaspoon salt
1 tablespoon mirin (sweet rice wine)
2 teaspoons curry powder
2 tablespoons cornstarch
1 tablespoon soy sauce

Cut fish into serving pieces; score lightly. Combine marinade ingredients and marinate fish 30 minutes. Dip fish into egg and dredge in cornflake crumbs or panko. Deep fry in oil heated to 365°F for 2 to 3 minutes on each side or until golden brown. Drain on absorbent paper.

VARIATION:
Substitute any white flesh fish for mahimahi.

- Rub thin-cut pork chops with salt and pepper. Brown in nonstick skillet on both sides. Add condensed cream of mushroom soup, 1 cup water, sliced onion and mushrooms; cover and simmer 30 to 45 minutes over low heat. Serve over steamed rice.

- Sauté peeled shrimp in large skillet in a little olive oil until just cooked. Stir in bottled pasta sauce; heat. Serve over cooked pasta.

- Brown chunks of boneless chicken, chopped onion, chopped bell pepper in large skillet in a little canola oil. Stir in 3 to 4 cups water and bring to a boil. Add chunks of carrots and/or potatoes, if desired; cook 20 minutes. Add pieces of curry sauce mix to pan and cook over low heat about 10 to 15 minutes or until thickened. Serve over cooked rice or pasta with minced green onion and desired condiments such as minced macadamia nuts, grated coconut, bacon bits, chutney, etc.

- Add corn and frozen shelled edamame to canned New England clam chowder. Top with crumbled precooked bacon and freshly ground pepper.

- Sauté sliced portobello mushrooms, peppers and sliced onions in olive oil. Roll in flour tortillas and serve with salsa and sour cream.

- Mix canned condensed cream of chicken soup with a little milk in large skillet until creamy. Stir in frozen mixed vegetables and cubed cooked chicken or turkey; heat until hot. Spoon over warmed biscuits.

- Heat frozen creamed spinach in microwave oven. Pour into a large nonstick skillet. Pour beaten eggs over spinach in skillet; cover and cook over low heat until eggs are set. Arrange ham slices on toasted English muffins; top with spinach and eggs.

- Fill split warmed pita bread with smoked turkey, roasted peppers, onion, watercress and humus.

- Sauté chicken tenders until cooked through. Serve with a dip made of orange marmalade, soy sauce and a bit of mustard.

- Spread whole grain bread slices with mustard. Top half the slices with sliced Brie cheese; broil until melted. Top other slices with sliced ham and alfalfa sprouts or arugula. Sandwich together.

(continued on the next page)

- Spread flour tortillas with Thousand Island dressing. Top with fresh corned beef slices, sliced Swiss cheese and deli coleslaw. Roll up; microwave 1 minute to melt cheese.

- Season scallops with salt and pepper. Sauté in a little olive oil in a large skillet just until cooked through. Remove. Add pesto and a bit of fat-free half-and-half to skillet; heat gently. Spoon onto plates; top with scallops.

- Marinate turkey or chicken cutlets in Italian dressing. Cook on range-top grill or broil until cooked through. Top with a mixture of baby arugula and halved grape tomatoes and thinly sliced red onion. Drizzle with more dressing to serve.

- Form ground pork into ½-inch thick patties. Cook in nonstick skillet until done. Stir in barbecue sauce; heat through. Serve on toasted buns with deli coleslaw.

- Brown ground beef in large skillet; stir in canned chunky tomatoes and green chilis, tomato sauce and chili seasoning mix. Simmer until slightly thickened; stir in canned corn and rinsed beans. Heat through. Great with rice or crackers.

- Brown lean ground beef or chicken with some minced fresh ginger and garlic. Season with soy sauce, rice vinegar and oyster sauce. Spoon into leaves of green leaf or iceberg lettuce; top with shredded carrot and chopped green onion.

- Heat refrigerated, fully cooked chicken nuggets in a nonstick skillet. Toss with salad greens, sliced sweet onions, cherry tomatoes and ranch dressing.

- Heat refrigerated or frozen, fully cooked chicken nuggets. Meanwhile, heat bottled sweet-sour sauce and drained canned pineapple chunks until hot. Toss with chicken nuggets and serve with hot steamed rice.

- Spread individual pre-baked pizza crusts with pesto. Layer with slices of plum tomatoes and fresh mozzarella. Bake at 450°F for 8 minutes or until cheese melts.

- Brown ham steak in nonstick skillet. Stir together hot pepper jelly, diced pineapple and chopped cilantro; spoon over ham. Serve with steamed green beans.

- Beat eggs in bowl; stir in chopped Portuguese sausage, tomatoes, green onions and cilantro. Scramble in nonstick skillet until of desired doneness. Serve on toasted and buttered whole wheat or Portuguese sweet bread.

- Place salmon fillets in 2-inch deep dish or pan. Pour hot boiling water over fillets to cover; seal immediately with aluminum foil and let stand 25 to 30 minutes or until fish is cooked through; drain. Combine heated salad oil, soy sauce, grated ginger and a little sugar; mix well and spoon over fish. Garnish with chopped green onion. Serve with hot steamed rice.

RICE & NOODLES

Rice is economical, delicious, nutritious, and versatile. It is without any doubt your most useful food. More than 7,000 varieties of rice are produced throughout the world but the most common are long-grain, medium-grain, short-grain, brown, regular milled white, precooked, parboiled, and wild rice.

The rice and noodle recipes in this section feature those that are most frequently requested because they are not only tasty but economical and easy to prepare. Hope you enjoy them!

Classic Fried Rice

Yield: 6 to 8 servings

There are many variations of Fried Rice. Use your creativity to develop your own special version just for your family.

3 tablespoons salad oil
¼ pound ham, pork, chicken or shrimp, minced
½ pound char siu, slivered
½ cup minced green onion
¾ cup frozen peas & carrots, cooked
6 cups cold cooked rice
2 eggs, beaten
¼ cup chopped Chinese parsley

Seasonings:
1 tablespoon soy sauce
1 tablespoon oyster sauce
½ teaspoon salt

Stir-fry meat in hot oil 1 minute. Stir in char siu, onion, peas and carrots; cook 30 seconds. Add rice and seasonings; stir-fry additional minute. Add beaten eggs and Chinese parsley; toss gently 1 minute or until eggs are cooked. Garnish with additional Chinese parsley or minced green onion, if desired.

Tori Gohan

Chicken-Rice

Yield: 4 to 6 servings

Save time and money with this one-pot rice dish.

1 dried shiitake mushroom
½ cup water
2 cups rice, washed and drained
1½ cups water
¼ cup sake (rice wine)
1 cup boneless chicken, sliced
½ cup carrot, slivered
2 teaspoons soy sauce
¼ teaspoon salt

Garnishes:
Chinese peas, blanched
Peas, cooked

Soak mushroom in ½ cup water to soften. Cut mushroom into slivers and combine with all the remaining ingredients, including mushroom liquid. Cover and cook over high heat until liquid comes to a boil. Reduce heat to simmer; cook until liquid is reduced to level of rice. Reduce heat to low and cook additional 15 minutes or until rice is cooked. Let stand 5 minutes before serving. Garnish with blanched Chinese peas or cooked peas, if desired.

Tasty Spam™ Mochi Rice

Yield: 6 servings

This recipe by Shayna Lum of Honolulu, Hawai'i won First Prize in the SPAM® recipe contest. Shayna adapted the recipe from one of her mom's and it is a hit with all of her friends. It is easy to prepare plus economical! Enjoy!!!

3 cups mochi rice
8 dried shiitake mushrooms
2 tablespoons dried shrimp, finely chopped
2 cups warm water
1 tablespoon salad oil
1 can SPAM®, diced
¼ cup Chinese parsley, chopped
¼ green onion, chopped
3 tablespoons oyster sauce

Wash mochi rice in colander until water runs clear; drain and pour into bowl. Add water to cover and soak overnight. Combine mushrooms, shrimp and water; let stand 1 hour.

Meanwhile, heat oil in nonstick pan and stir-fry SPAM® over medium heat until lightly browned, about 3 to 4 minutes; drain on absorbent paper and set aside.

Remove mushrooms and shrimp from water; reserve water and add enough water to make 1½ cups. Chop mushroom and shrimp. Drain rice and place in large microwave safe container. Add shrimp, mushrooms, fried SPAM®, Chinese parsley, green onion, oyster sauce and reserved water. Add more water, if necessary, until water is equal to level of rice. Cover and microwave on "high" for 7 minutes; stir. Cover and microwave on "high" additional 7 minutes; stir. Cover and cook another 5 minutes on "high"; stir. Continue to cover and microwave on "high" until rice is fully cooked, about 2 to 5 more minutes. Stir before serving.

TIP:
Microwave times may vary according to wattage. This recipe was based on a 1300 watt microwave.

Sushi Rice

Yield: 4 cups

Rice flavored delicately with sweetened rice vinegar is the basis of sushi. The origin of sushi goes back as far as the mid-sixth century Southeast Asia. It was not until the late 17th century that vinegar was added to the cooked rice to give it its characteristic acidic flavor.

1½ cups rice
1½ cups water
⅓ cup rice vinegar
⅓ cup sugar
½ teaspoon salt

In a rice cooker or 2-quart saucepan, rinse rice; drain. Add water and cook rice. While rice is cooking, combine vinegar, sugar, and salt in a small saucepan. Bring to a boil; cool. Reserve 1½ tablespoons of the vinegar mixture; pour remainder over hot rice, mixing lightly. Use reserved vinegar mixture for moistening hands or nori when making sushi.

Inari Sushi

Yield: 12 servings

Sushi rice mixed together with a variety of cooked vegetables is stuffed into deep-fried tofu pockets seasoned delicately to soy sauce and sugar.

6 aburage (fried tofu cones)
3 cups water
⅓ cup soy sauce
3 tablespoons sugar
1 teaspoon salt
3 dried mushrooms, soaked
⅓ cup finely chopped carrot
⅓ cup finely chopped green beans
4 cups Sushi Rice

Cut each aburage diagonally into halves to form two triangles. Remove soft inner portion of aburage; discard. In a saucepan, simmer aburage cones in 2 cups of the water for 15 minutes; drain. Add the remaining 1 cup water, the soy sauce, sugar, and salt to cones aburage simmer fop 10 minutes. Remove cones and save soy sauce mixture. Remove stems from mushrooms; finely chop caps. Cook mushrooms, carrot, and beans in the soy sauce mixture for 15 minutes or until tender; drain. Fold vegetables into Sushi Rice; loosely pack into seasoned aburage.

Spanish Rice

Yield: 8 to 10 servings

This popular school lunch rice dish is one that is very nostalgic to many as it evokes warm memories of "small-kid" time.

1 pound ground beef
1 pound ground pork
½ green pepper, chopped
1 medium onion, peeled and minced
1 rib celery, minced
3 cups beef broth or water
1 can (28 oz.) crushed tomatoes
1 can (15 oz.) whole peeled tomatoes
1 can (6 oz.) tomato paste
Salt and ground pepper to taste
2 teaspoons chili powder
1 teaspoon Worcestershire sauce, optional
2 cups uncooked rice
1½ cups minced ham or Portuguese sausage

Sauté ground beef and pork with bell pepper, onion and celery until onion is limp; drain. Place in large bowl; add broth or water, tomatoes, tomato paste and seasonings to meat mixture; stir in rice. Toss gently to combine. Place in 9 x 13-inch baking dish; sprinkle with ham or sausage over top and cover with foil. Bake. Temperature 325°F. Time: 45 to 60 minutes; uncover, cook additional 30 minutes or until rice is tender.

Korean-Style Fried Rice

Yield: 6 to 8 servings

¼ pound pork, thinly sliced
¼ teaspoon sesame seed oil
¼ teaspoon sugar
1½ tablespoons soy sauce
1 clove garlic, minced

2 tablespoons salad oil
1 pound bean sprouts, washed and
   drained
3 cups cold cooked rice
¼ cup kim chee, drained and finely
   chopped
3 tablespoons soy sauce
1 cup green onion, minced

Marinate pork in sesame seed oil, sugar, soy sauce and garlic for 15 minutes.

Stir-fry pork in hot oil for 2 to 3 minutes or until cooked through. Add bean sprouts, cooked rice and kim chee; stir-fry for 2 minutes or until rice is hot. Add soy sauce and green onion; stir-fry additional minute. Serve hot.

Bibimbap

Mixed Rice

Yield: 10 to 12 servings

This classic Korean meal-in-a-bowl features hot steaming rice topped with cooked vegetables and tasty slices of Korean barbecue beef.

2 tablespoons soy sauce
2 tablespoons toasted sesame seeds,
   crushed
1 teaspoon salad oil
1 teaspoon salt
1 teaspoon sugar
1 package (12 oz.) bean sprouts
1 bunch watercress, cut into 1-inch
   lengths
12 cups hot steamed rice
1 cup kim chee, drained and chopped
½ cup Bul Kogi (see page 40), cut into
   strips
1 tablespoon sesame oil
3 tablespoons soy sauce

Garnishes:
Fried egg strips
Finely minced green onions

Combine first 5 ingredients; add bean sprouts and watercress; cook over medium heat for 1 minute. Cool; squeeze out excess liquid; set aside.

In a large bowl, combine rice with remaining ingredients; toss gently. Add vegetables and toss until well mixed. Garnish with egg strips and onions to serve.

Baked Spaghetti

Yield: 4 to 6 servings

Pasta dishes are popular as suppertime standards for many. Tried-and-true simple recipes like this Baked Spaghetti becomes a new dish with your favorite "add-ins" such as chopped ham, prosciutto, bell pepper, etc.

1 tablespoon olive oil
1 cup minced round onion
1 large clove garlic, minced
1 pound lean ground beef, turkey or chicken
1 can (26½ oz.) spaghetti sauce
½ cup ketchup
1½ cups water
2 teaspoons sugar
½ teaspoon dried oregano
1 package (8 oz.) dried spaghetti noodles
1½ cups shredded Italian blend cheese

Heat oil in large skillet; sauté onion and garlic. Add ground meat and cook until lightly browned; drain excess oil. Add spaghetti sauce, water, sugar and oregano; bring to a simmer.

Spray 2-quart casserole with oil; pour in ½ cup sauce to cover bottom of casserole dish. Break uncooked spaghetti into thirds and lay half evenly in casserole dish. Pour half of remaining sauce over spaghetti; sprinkle with half of the cheese. Add remaining spaghetti and sauce; top with remaining cheese. Cover and bake. Temperature: 350°F. Time: 20 minutes. Uncover, bake additional 20 to 25 minutes or until cheese is light brown. Remove from oven; let stand 5 to 10 minutes before cutting to serve,

lasagna

Yield: 6 to 8 servings

Easy, never-fail recipes like this one are essential to family-pleasing meals. If you like it spicier, just add a cup of chopped Italian or Portuguese sausage with the beef.

½ cup chopped onion
1 clove garlic, minced
2 tablespoons salad oil
1 pound ground beef
2 cans tomato sauce
1 cup water
1 teaspoon salt
½ teaspoon oregano
¼ teaspoon pepper
½ teaspoon sugar
8 ounces lasagna noodles, cooked and
   drained
2 cups shredded cheddar or American
   cheese
8 ounces sliced mozzarella cheese

Sauté onion and garlic in hot oil. Add meat; brown. Add tomato sauce, water and seasonings; cover and simmer 20 minutes. Place half of noodles in bottom of 13 x 9-inch baking dish. Spread half of cheddar or American cheese over noodles. Top with half of mozzarella cheese slices and half of the meat sauce. Repeat layers. Bake. Temperature: 350°F. Time: 30 to 45 minutes.

VARIATION:
Cottage cheese and shredded Parmesan cheese may be used instead of cheddar or American cheese.

Chap Chae

Stir-Fried Vegetables with Long Rice

Yield: 6 to 8 servings

This Korean noodle dish is forever on the menu at every Korean restaurant. The variety of vegetables in it makes it especially tasty!

2 packages (1.75 oz. each) long rice
½ pound beef, cut into 1-inch strips
1 garlic, minced
2 tablespoons vegetable or sesame oil
6 dried shiitake mushrooms, softened in hot water; stems removed and caps cut into strips
1 medium carrot, julienned
½ bunch watercress, cut into 2-inch lengths
1 stalk celery, thinly slices
1 medium onion, sliced
½ pound green beans, French cut
3 tablespoons soy sauce
1½ tablespoons sugar
1¼ teaspoons salt
Dash of pepper
⅛ teaspoon monosodium glutamate (MSG), optional
¼ cup water

Garnishes:
¼ cup green onions, chopped
Fried egg strips

Soak long rice in hot water for 20 minutes; cut bundles of long rice in half and cook in 1½ quarts of boiling water for 1 minute or until translucent; drain thoroughly. Set aside.

In a large skillet, stir-fry beef and garlic in hot oil for 1 minute. Add vegetables; Sauté for 2 minutes. Combine soy sauce, sugar, salt, pepper, MSG and water in a bowl. Stir long rice and soy sauce mixture into vegetables; cook for 1 to 2 minutes, stirring occasionally.

Garnish with green onions and fried egg strips to serve.

TIP:
Long rice, also known as cellophane or beanthread noodles are made from the starch of the mung bean. Almost clear after being heated they are flavorless and take on the taste of the sauce in which they are cooked and should be softened in water before being used.

Chicken Long Rice

Yield: 8 to 10 servings

1 1½ to 2½ pound frying chicken
3½-inch slices ginger root
2½ teaspoons salt
4 cups water
1 4-ounce bundle long rice
¼ cup chopped green onion
¼ teaspoon white pepper

Cover chicken with 4 cups water; add ginger and 1 teaspoon salt. Simmer until chicken is tender (about 45 to 60 minutes). Cool. Bone chicken and cut into bite-size pieces.

Cover long rice with warm water and let stand ½ hour; drain and cut in 4-inch lengths.

Remove ginger from broth. Add long rice, green onion, remaining salt, pepper, and chicken. Bring to a boil and simmer 10 minutes. Garnish with additional chopped green onion, if desired.

Chow Fun

Yield: about 8 servings

My grandchildren love chow fun. It's quick to prepare and very versatile as the ingredients can be tailored to your own taste.

3 sheets fresh look fun noodles
3 tablespoons salad oil
½ pound char siu, slivered
1 small onion, sliced
1 small carrot, slivered
3 tablespoons soy sauce
2 tablespoons oyster sauce
1¼ teaspoons salt
¼ teaspoon sugar
¼ teaspoon fresh ground pepper
¼ pound Chinese peas, washed and strings removed
1 package (12 oz.) bean sprouts, washed and drained
¼ cup chopped green onion

Chinese parsley, optional

Slice look fun noodles into ½-inch strips. Heat salad oil in wok or large skillet; stir-fry char siu for 30 seconds. Add onion, carrot; stir-fry 30 seconds. Stir in look fun and soy sauce, oyster sauce, salt, sugar and pepper. Stir in Chinese peas and bean sprouts; stir-fry additional 30 seconds. Add green onion just before serving. Garnish with Chinese parsley, if desired.

Classic Macaroni & Cheese

Yield: 4 to 6 servings

This wonderful comfort food is delicious as is, but if you want to kick it up a notch, try one of the variations below.

1 package (7 oz.) uncooked elbow, rotini or ziti macaroni
2 tablespoons butter or margarine
¼ cup chopped onion
2 tablespoons flour
1 teaspoon Dijon mustard
½ teaspoon salt
¼ teaspoon pepper
2 cups milk
1 cup grated extra-sharp white cheddar cheese
½ cup grated Monterey Jack cheese

Cook pasta according to package directions. Heat butter or margarine in 3-quart saucepan over medium heat. Add onion and cook about 3 minutes. Stir in flour, mustard, salt and pepper. Cook, stirring constantly until mixture is bubbly; remove from heat. Stir in milk, whisking constantly; heat to boiling. Reduce heat to simmer, and cook 1 minute, stirring constantly. Remove from heat. Stir in cheeses until melted. Add macaroni and stir until coated. Pour pasta into ungreased 1½ quart casserole and spread evenly. Bake. Temperature: 375°F. Time: 25 minutes or until bubbly and light brown.

VARIATIONS:
- **Bacon Or Pancetta Mac 'N Cheese:** Add crumbled bacon or pancetta to the sauce along with the pasta.

- **Ham Mac 'N Cheese:** Add 1 cup diced cooked ham to the sauce along with the pasta.

- **Hot Mac 'N Cheese:** Add ¼ to ½ teaspoon crushed red pepper flakes with the mustard.

Pansit

Filipino-Style Fried Noodles

Yield: 4 to 6 servings

½ pound rice noodles (bijon or rice sticks)
3 tablespoons salad oil
2 cloves garlic, crushed
¾ pound pork, cut in thin strips
½ pound boneless chicken, cut in thin strips
¼ pound shrimp, cleaned and diced
½ cup sliced celery
Dash of ground pepper

Garnishes:
½ cup green onion, chopped
3 limes, quartered
3 hard-cooked eggs, quartered

Soak rice noodles in cold water for 30 minutes or until softened. Sauté garlic in oil until slightly browned; remove. Add pork and sauté over medium heat, stirring frequently, about 4 minutes. Add chicken and sauté 2 to 3 minutes. Add shrimp and sauté 2 to 3 minutes. Stir in celery, salt and pepper; cook additional minute.

Drain rice noodles and cut into 4-inch lengths. Add to meat mixture and continue cooking, stirring frequently, until noodles are heated through, 2 to 3 minutes. Place on large serving platter. Sprinkle with green onions and arrange alternate wedges of lime and egg around. Serve hot with lime juice and soy sauce.

VARIATIONS:
Add-in: Chopped ham, proscuitto, Italian or Portuguese sausage, bell pepper, mushrooms, basil.

Pho

Vietnamese Rice Noodles in Beef Broth

Yield: 4 servings

This Vietnamese soup consisting of rice noodles in a light beef based broth with the balanced flavors of salty, spicy, and citrus is highly addictive. Pho usually becomes an instant favorite for anyone who tastes it.

1 pound ⅛-inch wide dried rice sticks

Broth:
4 pounds beef soup bones
2 gallons water plus more as needed
1 large onion
1 piece (3 oz.) fresh ginger, washed and crushed
1 turnip, washed and peeled
1 carrot, washed and peeled
2 pounds beef flank
1 pound beef sirloin
6 pieces star anise
2 teaspoons salt
½ cup nuoc mam (fish sauce)

Garnishes:
2 scallions, thinly sliced
2 medium onion, sliced paper thin
1 tablespoon Chinese parsley (cilantro)

Suggested Condiments:
2 cups fresh bean sprouts, washed and drained
2 fresh red chili peppers, sliced
2 limes, wedged
1 bunch fresh mint, washed and drained
1 bunch fresh basil, washed and drained
Hot chili-garlic sauce
Hoisin (brown soy bean) sauce

Place beef bones in large stock pot; add enough water to cover bones; bring to a boil and boil for 5 minutes. Drain and rinse bones and stock pot. Return bones to stock pot; add 2 gallons water; bring to a boil and skim fat from surface as necessary. Simmer over low heat for 45 to 60 minutes.

Meanwhile, char onion and ginger directly over open flame, if possible, until the flavors are released. Place the whole onion, ginger, turnip, carrot, beef flank, sirloin, star anise and tendon in stock pot adding more water, if necessary, to cover. Simmer for additional 2 hours, adding more water, if necessary. Remove beef and tendon; cool slightly and slice into serving pieces; set aside. When the broth is ready, strain. Add salt and nuoc mam and adjust taste, if necessary; bring to a boil again.

Soak rice sticks in warm water for 30 minutes; drain and set aside. In a separate pot, bring 4 quarts of water to a boil; add softened rice sticks and drain immediately. Divide noodles into 4 large bowls; top with sliced beef and tendon. Ladle boiling broth directly over the meat; garnish with scallions, onion slices and Chinese parsley. Serve with desired condiments, hot garlic-chili and hoisin sauce.

VARIATION:
Substitute paper-thin slices of raw beef, cooked chicken or pork for cooked beef and tendon.

Saimin

Yield: 2 to 3 servings

Saimin represents a third-stage evolution. In the beginning, there was mein—Chinese noodles. Then came the Japanese adaptation—ramen. In Hawai'i, the chewy noodles in broth became saimin.

The first saimin recipes show up in local cookbooks in the 1930s; the first vendors were Japanese immigrants who sold their noodles from pushcarts, often set up outside gas stations. Garnished with char siu, green onion, and maybe a few strips of fried egg, saimin is for many of us a warm bowl of slurpy comfort.

1 (9.7 oz) package fresh saimin or ramen noodles

Saimin Dashi:
(Yield: 4 servings)

2 quarts water
½ cup dried shrimp
1 piece (2 x 6-inch) dashi konbu
2 teaspoons salt
2 teaspoons soy sauce
½ teaspoon monosodium glutamate (MSG), optional

Condiments:
Kamaboko slices
Luncheon meat, cut into strips
Char siu, cut into slices or strips
Fried egg strips
Minced green onion

Prepare noodles per package directions. To prepare broth, combine water with dried shrimps and konbu. Bring water to a boil; remove konbu. Simmer remaining mixture over low heat for 40 to 60 minutes. Discard shrimp. Add remaining seasonings; adjust taste as necessary. Pour over cooked noodles; garnish with desired condiments.

Hiya Ramen

Cold Saimin

Yield: 4 to 6 servings

1 package dried or raw saimin noodles

Tsukejiru (Dipping Saimin):
½ cup rice vinegar
½ cup shoyu
½ cup supr
¼ teaspoon sesame seed oil
1 package dashi-no-moto
Few drops hot sauce, optional

Gu (Condiments):
1 small cucumber, slivered
2 cups bean sprouts, blanched
1 cup minced green onion
1 cup luncheon meat, slivered
1 tablespoon toasted sesame seeds
Fried egg strips

Cook saimin as directed on package. Rinse, drain and chill. Arrange noodles in individual serving bowls (on ice, if desired); arrange Gu over noodles.

To prepare Tsukejiru, combine ingredients in a jar; shake thoroughly. Pour over arrangement of noodles and condiments to serve.

Gon Lo Mein

Chinese-Style Fried Noodles

Yield: 4 to 6 servings

1 tablespoon salad oil
½ cup boneless chicken, slivered
½ cup char siu, slivered
¼ cup bamboo shoots, sliced
½ cup celery, sliced diagonally
½ cup green onion, cut in 1½-inch lengths
1 package (12 oz.) bean sprouts
1 tablespoon toasted sesame seeds
1 pound fresh fried noodles (chow mein)

Seasonings:
2 teaspoons oyster sauce
½ cup chicken broth
1 teaspoon salt
2 tablespoons toasted sesame seeds

Garnishes:
¼ cup Chinese parsley (cilantro)
¼ cup char siu (sweet roast pork), slivered

Stir-fry chicken in hot oil for 2 minutes. Add char siu; stir-fry additional minute. Add bamboo shoots, celery, green onion, bean sprouts, sesame seeds, noodles and seasonings. Stir-fry additional minute to heat through. Garnish with Chinese parsley and char siu.

FAMILY FAVORITES

There is nothing like sharing homemade dishes with those you care about, so check out some of the easy-to-prepare dishes from across generations of my family that are economical and delicious. On special occasions I cooked and shared some of the dishes of my heritage with my colleagues at Columbia University in NYC while a graduate student in the 1950s. These are still my go-to treasured family recipes today.

Recipes passed down in families are still the best kind as they hold cherished memories.

Cucumber Namasu

Yield: 3 to 4 servings

Namasu is a classic Japanese salad and you can create your own variations. Namasu was always on the menu for family dinners.

1 cucumber
2 tablespoons shredded carrot
2 stalks celery, optional
¼ teaspoon salt

<u>Vinegar Sauce:</u>
5 tablespoons sugar
¼ teaspoon salt
¼ cup rice vinegar or lemon juice

2 radishes, thinly sliced

Cut cucumber in half lengthwise. Slice cucumber and celery into thin diagonal pieces. Sprinkle with salt. Let stand 10 minutes; rinse salt off; drain, then squeeze out excess water.

Combine ingredients for Vinegar Sauce; pour over vegetables and mix. Garnish with thinly sliced radishes.

VARIATIONS:
- Add cooked minced clams, shrimp or fishcake
- Drain a can of sliced beets; pour Vinegar Sauce over
- Substitute blanched bean sprouts for cucumbers

Tsukemono No Moto

Japanese Pickling Brine

Yield: 2 cups

Vegetables preserved in bring (tsukemono) are generally served as a side dish in the typical Japanese meal. Though every family has its own favorite recipe for tsukemono, we'd like to share my mother's with you.

1¾ cups water
1 piece (5-inch) dashi konbu
2 tablespoons rock salt
1½ tablespoons sugar
½ teaspoon soy sauce
1½ teaspoons rice vinegar
1½ teaspoons sake
¼ teaspoon monosodium glutamate (MSG), optional

Suggested vegetable to pickle: Turnips, radishes, head cabbage, cucumbers, eggplants, celery cabbage, Chinese mustard cabbage

Combine all ingredients for Tsukemono No Moto of your choice and add desired vegetables. Let stand 1 to 2 days in refrigerator or at room temperature with 3 to 5 pound weight. Serve with soy sauce.

Chicken Katsu

Chicken Cutlet

Yield: 6 servings

Drizzled with a slightly spicy Katsu Sauce, this moist and flavorful crispy coated fried chicken is one of my grandson's favorite island dishes.

2 pounds boneless chicken breasts, skin removed
½ cup flour
2 eggs, beaten
2 cups panko (bread crumbs)
Oil for frying

Katsu Sauce (see page 154)

Dredge chicken in flour, dip in eggs, and coat with panko; refrigerate for 15 to 20 minutes. Fry cutlets in oil heated to 375°F until golden brown; drain on absorbent paper. Cut into 1-inch strips and serve with Katsu Sauce.

VARIATION:
Pork or beef may be substituted for chicken.

Teriyaki Spam™ Musubi

Yield: 18 musubi

A favorite for picnics and gatherings in Hawai'i that really needs no recipe. My daughter introduced Spam™ Musubi to my grandson's tae kwan do team on the East Coast and it caught on like wildfire!

**2 cans (12 oz. size) SPAM®,
   cut in 18 slices total**
18 cups cooked rice
1 bottle (½-oz.) furikake, optional
10 sheets nori, cut in half

Teriyaki Sauce:
½ cup soy sauce
½ cup brown sugar, packed
**3 tablespoons mirin (sweet rice wine) or
   water**
1¼ inch piece fresh ginger, optional
1 clove garlic, minced

Combine all ingredients for teriyaki sauce in jar; cover and shake vigorously; set aside.

Fry SPAM® in nonstick skillet until lightly browned; pour teriyaki sauce over and cook 1 minute. Drain and set aside to cool. Mix hot rice with furikake; cool.

Lay a piece of nori flat on work surface. Center a SPAM® musubi mold over nori. Fill musubi mold ¾ way up with rice; top with SPAM®. Press down firmly into mold; remove mold. Fold nori over SPAM® and seal. Cool; cut musubi in half.

VARIATIONS:
- Omelet Musubi: Scramble 2 to 3 large eggs with 1 teaspoon soy sauce. Cook in hot oil in skillet until well done; slice to fit musubi mold. Substitute omelet for SPAM®.
- Teri-Beef: Cook beef slices in teriyaki sauce; substitute for SPAM®. Drain well before placing on rice.
- Teri-Chicken: Cook boneless chicken breast cutlets in teriyaki sauce; substitute for SPAM®. Drain well before placing on rice.

Prune Mui

Yield: about 3 quarts

Onolicious! Great substitute recipe for the Chinese preserved plums.

5 pounds dried pitted prunes
½ pound dried lemon peel, chopped
½ pound li hing mui
1 pound dark brown sugar
1½ cups lemon juice
¼ cup whiskey
3 tablespoons rock salt
1 tablespoon Chinese five spice powder
8 whole cloves

Combine prunes, lemon peel and li hing mui in a large bowl. Combine remaining ingredients and pour over prunes, mixing thoroughly. Let stand 2 to 3 days before serving.

Shari's Skillet Spaghetti

Yield: 4 servings

This is one of my daughter's go-to recipes for its easy to prepare, inexpensive, and tasty!

1 pound ground beef
2 tablespoons salad oil
⅓ cup finely chopped onion
⅓ cup finely chopped green pepper
1 No. 303 can tomatoes and juice
½ cup tomato ketchup
½ teaspoon salt
¼ teaspoon pepper
1 tablespoon Worcestershire sauce
½ cup water
6 ounces spaghetti noodles, broken into
   1-inch pieces

Brown ground beef in hot salad oil in skillet. Add remaining ingredients; mix well. Cover and simmer for 45 minutes or until spaghetti is cooked.

Alissa's Chocolate Chip Cookies

Yield: About 5 dozen

The original chocolate chip cookie, Toll House Cookie, got its name from a lovely old tollhouse owned by Mr. & Mrs. Wakefield who turned the historic old house into the now-famous Toll House Inn located between Boston and New Bedford, Massachusetts. Mrs. Wakefield first baked the original Toll House Cookies for guests at the Inn. Since then, there have been many variations.

1 cup butter or margarine, softened
¾ cup sugar
¾ cup light brown sugar, packed
2 eggs, beaten
1 teaspoon vanilla extract
2¼ cups flour
1 teaspoon baking soda
1 teaspoon salt
2 cups (12 ounce package) semi-sweet chocolate chips

In a large mixing bowl, cream butter or margarine with sugars until light and fluffy. Add eggs and vanilla; beat well. Combine flour, baking soda, and salt; mix well and gradually mix into creamed mixture. Stir in choco late chips. Drop by rounded tablespoon onto ungreased baking sheets. Bake. Temperature 375°F. Time: 9 to 11 minutes or until golden brown. Let stand 1 to 2 minutes; remove to wire racks to cool completely. Store in airtight container.

VARIATIONS:

- Hawaiian Chocolate Chip: Add 1 cup chopped macadamia nuts and 1 cup shredded coconut to Chocolate Chip Cookie recipe. Yield: About 5-½ dozen.

- Chocolate Chip Bars: Prepare dough as directed above; spread into 9 x 13 x 2-inch pan. Bake. Time: 20 to 25 minutes or until golden brown. Cool in pan; cut into bars. Yield: About 24 to 30 bars.

An Da Gi
Japanese Doughnut

Yield: 2½ to 3 dozen

WOW! Fresh, hot and tasty homemade doughnuts at a moment's notice! Try it, you'll love it!

3 cups flour
1 cup sugar
4½ teaspoons baking powder
½ teaspoon salt
3 eggs, slightly beaten
1 cup milk

Sift dry ingredients together. Combine eggs and milk; add to dry ingredients. Mix thoroughly. Drop by teaspoonfuls into oil heated to 375°F. Cook about 2 minutes, or until golden brown. Drain on paper towel and 1 roll in sugar, if desired.

Snickerdoodles

Yield: about 4 dozen

The grandkids love these old-time favorite cookies with delicious cinnamon-sugar coating sprinkled on top...good especially with cold milk or hot tea.

1 cup butter or margarine, softened
1½ cups sugar
2 eggs, beaten
1 teaspoon vanilla extract
2¾ cups flour
2 teaspoons baking powder
½ teaspoon salt
2 teaspoons cinnamon
3 tablespoons sugar

Cream butter or margarine with sugar until light and fluffy. Add eggs and vanilla; beat well. Mix together flour, baking powder, and salt; add to creamed mixture and mix thoroughly. Chill dough 1 hour. Form dough into walnut-size balls. In small bowl, mix together cinnamon and sugar; roll dough in mixture to coat. Place 2 inches apart on lightly greased baking sheets. Bake. Temperature: 375°F. Time: 10 to 12 minutes or until golden brown. Cool completely and store in airtight container.

Oatmeal Cookies

Yield: about 5 dozen

There is nothing my granddaughter, Alissa, likes more than "plain old-fashioned" Oatmeal Cookies for an after-school snack or a dessert after a hearty dinner. Yummy! It's even better with raisins and nuts for a wholesome treat.

1 cup butter or vegetable shortening, softened
1 cup brown sugar, packed
½ cup sugar
1 egg
¼ cup water
¾ teaspoon vanilla extract
3 cups oatmeal (quick or old-fashioned, uncooked)
1 cup flour
1 teaspoon salt
½ teaspoon baking soda

Beat together butter or shortening, sugars, egg, water, and vanilla until creamy. Combine oats, flour, salt, and baking soda; stir into creamed mixture; mix well. Drop by rounded teaspoonfuls onto nonstick or ungreased cookie sheet. Bake. Temperature: 350°F. Time: 12 to 15 minutes or until light brown. Cool. These cookies keep well for a few weeks if stored in tightly covered container.

VARIATIONS:

- **Wholesome Oatmeal Cookies:** Add 1½ cups of any combination of the following to Oatmeal Cookie dough: Raisins, chopped nuts, coconut, craisins, or chocolate chips. Proceed as above.
- **Oatmeal Raisin Cookies:** Add 1½ cups of raisins to Oatmeal Cookie dough. Proceed as above.
- **Giant Oatmeal Cookies:** Drop dough by tablespoonfuls onto cookie sheet. Bake. Temperature: 375°F. Time: 12 to 15 minutes. Yield: about 2½ dozen

Stephen's Microwave Chichi Dango

Yield: about 20 pieces

This is one of my grandson's Stephen's favorite snacks and probably one of the first things he learned to make. He is becoming quite a "home chef" these days.

1½ cups mochiko (rice flour)
1 cup sugar
1½ cups water
½ teaspoon vanilla extract
Drop red (to make pink) or blue food coloring
Katakuriko (potato starch)

Mix mochiko and sugar together. In separate bowl mix together water or coconut milk, vanilla, and food coloring. Add liquid mixture slowly to dry ingredients and mix together until batter is smooth.

Pour into microwave tube pan or square microwave-safe glass dish sprayed lightly with vegetable oil. Seal tightly with plastic wrap. Microwave on medium for 6 to 7 minutes, then on high for 2 to 3 more minutes.

Carefully uncover immediately, being careful of steam; cool 10 to 15 minutes. Sprinkle surface with katakuriko, then remove from pan and cut into desired shapes with plastic knife. Roll in katakuriko before serving or packing.

VARIATIONS:
- **Liliko'i Mochi:** Substitute thawed frozen liliko'i concentrate diluted with water for coconut milk.
- **Guava Mochi:** Substitute thawed frozen guava concentrate diluted with water for coconut milk.

SALADS & SALAD DRESSINGS

Cooking is about ease and simplicity with today's hectic lifestyle and nothing fits that criteria more than a big, healthy salad. All you need are ultra-fresh greens and produce, perhaps a pantry staple or two and most important—a flavorful, homemade dressing.

Select an array of greens with different textures and flavors to add a "kick" to every mouthful, then add a dressing to match your flavor profile. Heavy cream dressings need sturdier leaves to cling to and vinaigrettes and light creamy dressings go well with leaves that are tender and only slightly spicy like arugula.

Greens must be thoroughly washed, well-chilled, and crisp! Choose other ingredients with an eye to overall color and texture, then apply the dressing, sparingly, with a well-balanced hand.

Salad Greens

A combination of greens—mix to your taste—and a combination of dressings (i.e., French with a dollop of mayonnaise, Italian with a dash of sour cream) place your signature firmly on each salad you serve. Look for these greens at your market to add flavor and interest to your salads:

Arugula	Leaf Lettuce	Beet Greens
Manoa Lettuce	Bibb Lettuce	Mizuna
Bok Choy	Red Cabbage	Boston Lettuce
Red Tip Leaf Lettuce	Cabbage	Romaine
Chinese Cabbage	Spinach	Curly Endive or Chicory
Swiss Chard	Escarole	Watercress
Iceberg Lettuce		

Prepare greens by washing each leaf with cool water. Drain in colander or salad basket. Store in plastic bag in refrigerator. Be sure leaves are completely drip-dried before tossing with dressing.

SALAD TIPS

- Mix marinated artichokes (with marinade), vegetables of your choice and chopped olives for a quick salad. Cooked pasta or torn greens may be added to stretch the salad.

- Add instant crunch texture to any salad by tossing or topping with nuts, canned chow mein noodles, or strips of fried won ton wrappers.

- Mix your favorite cooked pasta with bottled salad dressing plus your favorite vegetables, cheeses, and meats.

- For a quick, low-calorie main dish salad, arrange fresh or canned fruits and low-fat cottage cheese on a plate.

- Store watercress, parsley, and fresh herbs in screw-top jars filled with about an inch of water in the refrigerator with the stems in the water.

- Romaine and iceberg lettuce keep nicely in the refrigerator up to a week. Most other greens wilt within a few days of purchasing.

- To unmold your salad from its mold, just dip the mold into warm water for a few seconds to loosen the salad; center a plate upside down over the mold. Hold the mold and plate together and invert then shake gently until salad is loosened.

- Mix chilled leftover cooked vegetables with bottle salad dressings for a last-minute salad.

- Toss fresh or frozen (thawed and drained) fruits with equal parts apple juice and honey for a quick 'n easy fruit dressing.

SALADS

The salad greens are often referred to as the "filler" in a salad but it can be the main event by selecting an array of greens with different textures and flavors to add a "kick" to every mouthful. Top the salad with various produce and condiments to make it even more interesting and drizzle lightly with your homemade dressing of choice for a balanced mix of texture and flavors.

Macaroni–Potato Salad

Yield: 4 to 6 servings

A party in Hawai'i just isn't a party without macaroni salad…its flavor blends well with anything that is served!

½ cup minced round onion
½ cup minced celery
2 tablespoons sweet pickle relish, optional
¼ cup minced parsley
¼ cup minced kamaboko, optional
3 cups cooked elbow macaroni, well-drained and chilled
1½ cups cooked potato, cubed
1½ cups mayonnaise
½ teaspoon salt
⅛ teaspoon pepper

Combine onion, celery, pickle relish, parsley, kamaboko and potato with macaroni. Toss lightly. Add remaining ingredients; toss. Adjust seasonings to taste. Chill. Serve on bed of greens.

Tofu Salad

Yield: 6 to 8 servings

1 block firm tofu, drained and cubed
1 can (16 oz.) salmon, drained and flaked
1 large tomato, diced
½ small sweet onion, chopped or thinly
  sliced
1 package (12 oz.) bean sprouts
1 bunch watercress, cut into 1½ -inch
  piece
¼ cup green onion, chopped

Dressing:
½ cup canola oil
2 cloves garlic, minced
¼ cup soy sauce
¼ cup minced green onion

On a large platter, arrange ingredients in layers in the following order: watercress, bean sprouts, tofu, salmon, tomato, onion and green onion; chill.

To prepare dressing, combine oil and garlic in saucepan; cook until garlic begins to sizzle. Remove from heat; mix in soy sauce and green onion. Pour dressing over salad and serve immediately.

Tofu–Salmon Salad

Yield: 10 to 12 servings

A healthy fresh vegetable salad topped with tofu and salmon drizzled with light soy sauce dressing.

1 bunch watercress, washed and cut into 1½-inch lengths
1 package (12 oz.) bean sprouts, washed
1 block firm tofu, drained and cubed
1 can (1 pound) salmon, drained and flaked
1 firm ripe tomato, diced
1 small sweet Maui onion, thinly sliced
½ cup minced green onion

Dressing:
1 tablespoon canola oil
1 clove garlic, pressed
½ teaspoon grated fresh ginger root
⅓ cup soy sauce
2 teaspoons toasted sesame seeds

Layer watercress, bean sprouts, tofu, salmon, tomato, round and green onions on large platter. Combine Dressing ingredients in jar; cover and shake well then pour over salad just before serving. Garnish with additional toasted seeds, if desired.

Cobb Salad

Yield: 3 to 4 servings

The story goes that the original Cobb Salad was made famous in the 1930s by the Brown Derby in Hollywood and it is enjoying a renaissance today as many restaurants have it on the menu.

1 medium iceberg lettuce, shredded
⅓ cup white wine vinegar
¼ teaspoon garlic powder
¼ teaspoon fresh ground pepper
2 tablespoons snipped chives
½ cup olive oil
1 tomato, seeded and chopped
1½ cups cooked and diced chicken
1 medium avocado, pitted, peeled, diced
    and tossed with
1 tablespoon lemon juice
1 pound sliced bacon, cooked and
    crumbled
2 hard-cooked eggs, chopped
½ cup crumbled blue cheese

Arrange lettuce in large, wide salad bowl. In small bowl, whisk together vinegar, garlic powder, pepper, chives and oil; season to taste with salt. Pour over lettuce; toss to mix. Arrange tomato, chicken, avocado, bacon and eggs in separate wedge-shaped section on top of lettuce. Sprinkle with cheese; toss just before serving.

Somen Salad

Yield: 6 to 8 servings

Sauce:
⅓ cup sugar
1 cup dashi or chicken broth
⅓ cup soy sauce
⅓ cup rice vinegar
1 tablespoon sesame oil

1 package (9 oz.) dry somen noodles
3 cups shredded head lettuce
½ block (7 oz.) kamaboko, slivered
¼ pound char siu, slivered
1 small cucumber, slivered
¼ cup minced green onion
½ cup kizami nori (seasoned seaweed
    strips)
Fried egg strips

To prepare sauce, combine sugar, dashi or broth, soy sauce, vinegar and sesame oil in saucepan; bring to a boil and simmer 3 to 4 minutes over low heat. Chill.

Meanwhile, cook somen noodles according to package directions; rinse with cold water; drain and chill. Just before serving, arrange cold somen on bed of shredded lettuce; garnish with kamaboko, char siu, cucumber, green onion, nori and egg strips. Pour chilled sauce over to serve.

Caesar Salad

Yield: 4 to 6 servings

The Caesar Salad is said to have been created by an Italian chef and restaurant owner, Caesar Cardini, in 1924. There are countless variations of this classic salad but this one, using the coddled egg, is said to be a close adaptation of the original.

1 clove garlic, cut in half
4 anchovy fillets, chopped
⅓ cup olive oil
¼ cup fresh lemon juice
1 egg, coddled
1 teaspoon Worcestershire sauce
10 cups (1 to 2 heads) romaine lettuce,
   cut into bite-sized pieces
1 cup croutons
⅓ cup grated Parmesan or Romano
   cheese
Salt and fresh ground pepper to taste

Rub large wooden salad bowl with garlic. Mix together anchovies, oil, lemon juice, egg, Worcestershire sauce in salad bowl. Add chilled lettuce and toss gently until leaves are coated. Sprinkle with salt, pepper, croutons and cheese; toss and serve immediately.

VARIATIONS:

- Chicken Caesar Salad: Arrange 1 cup cooked chicken slices over lettuce
- Shrimp Caesar: Arrange 1 cup cooked and shelled shrimp over lettuce

Creamy Coleslaw

Yield: 4 to 6 servings

1 cup sour cream
¼ cup cider vinegar
½ teaspoon salt
¼ teaspoon white pepper
¼ cup sugar
1 quart chopped, crisp cabbage
Paprika

Combine sour cream, vinegar, salt, pepper and sugar; mix thoroughly. Pour over cabbage, sprinkle with paprika and toss gently. Serve on bed of lettuce.

Sigumchi Namul

Spinach Salad

Yield: 4 servings

1 bunch spinach, washed and blanched 2
   tablespoons soy sauce
1 tablespoon vinegar
¼ teaspoon sesame seed oil
1 tablespoon minced green onions
1½ teaspoons toasted sesame seeds,
   ground

Drain spinach well and squeeze out excess water; cut into 1½-inch lengths; set aside. Combine remaining ingredients and mix to combine; Add spinach and mix by hand while gently rubbing seasonings into the spinach.

Chinese Chicken Salad

Yield: 6 to 8 servings

It was around 1970 that this salad started to gain popularity. You'll find numerous variations of this popular salad which can be taken on a picnic or served at a dinner party.

1 medium head iceberg lettuce, shredded
2 romaine lettuce leaves, chopped
½ cup minced green onion
½ cup chopped Chinese parsley (cilantro)
1 package (3 oz.) fried won ton strips
¼ cup chopped roasted peanuts
1 pound cooked boneless chicken, shredded
½ cup char siu, slivered

Dressing:
2 tablespoons toasted sesame seeds
1 teaspoon salt
½ teaspoon pepper
¼ cup sugar
⅓ cup rice vinegar
¼ cup canola oil

Combine lettuce, green onion and Chinese parsley in large, chilled salad bowl; toss gently to mix. Sprinkle with won ton strips, peanuts, chicken and char siu.

Combine dressing ingredients in jar; cover and shake vigorously. Toss with vegetables or serve on the side with salad.

VARIATION:
Chinese Crab Salad: Substitute 1 cup cooked crab meat for chicken.

SALAD DRESSINGS

Skip the bottled dressings and instead, turn to one of these delicious dressings in this section that can be whipped up in minutes. They're great on salad greens and everything from chicken wings to shrimp!

Homemade dressings will stay delicious in your refrigerator for about 3 to 5 days.

Tomato Soup Dressing

Yield: ½ pint

1 can condensed tomato soup
½ cup sugar
½ cup vinegar
½ cup salad oil
1 teaspoon Worcestershire sauce
1 teaspoon dry mustard
1 tablespoon grated onion
1 small clove garlic, minced

Combine all ingredients in a jar; cover and shake vigorously. Refrigerate.

TIP:
To help prevent a greenish ring around the yolk when eggs are cooked in the shell, cool them immediately in cold running water.

Favorite French Dressing

Yield: 1½ cups

¼ cup brown or white sugar
½ teaspoon dry mustard
Dash of pepper
¼ teaspoon celery salt, if desired
½ teaspoon salt
¼ to ½ teaspoon Worcestershire sauce
½ cup ketchup
¾ cup salad oil
¼ cup vinegar
¼ cup chopped onion

Combine ingredients. Chill. Shake well before using.

Wikiwiki French Dressing

Yield: 2 cups

2 teaspoons salt
1 teaspoon sugar
½ teaspoon white pepper
1 teaspoon paprika
½ cup vinegar or lemon juice
1½ cups salad oil

Combine all ingredients in a covered jar. Chill. Cover and shake well before using.

This dressing is used as the basis of many other delicious dressings

Miso Dressing

Yield: about 2½ cups

A unique dressing for salads that's also great as a dip for fresh veggies.

1 cup canola oil
¼ cup sesame oil
1 clove garlic
1 tablespoon chopped round onion
¼ cup toasted sesame seeds
¾ cup sugar
3 tablespoons miso (soy bean paste)
1 tablespoon lime juice
1 teaspoon dry mustard
½ cup mayonnaise

Blend all ingredients in a blender or food processor. Store in covered jar in refrigerator until ready for use.

DRESSINGS OF CHOICE

TO MAKE THESE DRESSINGS	START WITH WIKIWIKI FRENCH DRESSING (see page 125)	ADD	ESPECIALLY GOOD WITH THESE SALADS
Blue Cheese	½ cup	2 tablespoons crumbed blue cheese	Head lettuce Tomatoes and greens
Celery Seed	½ cup	1 tablespoon ketchup 2 teaspoons sugar ¼ teaspoon celery seed 1 clove garlic, crushed	Vegetable
Chiffonade	1 cup	1 hard-cooked egg, chopped 1 small beet, finely chopped 1 small onion, finely chopped Hearts of lettuce	Cabbage Tomato
Chive	½ cup	1 to 2 tablespoons finely cut chives	Tuna Mixed greens Potato
Creamy	½ cup, made with lemon juice	⅓ cup light cream— add gradually, beat with rotary beater until thick	Fruit Chicken Potato
Creole	½ cup, made with lemon juice	¼ cup tomato ketchup ½ teaspoon Worcestershire sauce Dash hot sauce	Vegetable Meat Fish
Ginger	½ cup	1 tablespoon chopped crystallized ginger	Fruit
Mixed Garden	½ cup	1 teaspoon celery seed 2 teaspoons finely chopped onion 2 tablespoons finely chopped green pepper	Vegetable
Vinaigrette	½ cup	2 hard-cooked egg yolks, mashed 2 tablespoons chopped green pepper 1 tablespoon chopped onion	Vegetable

SAVORY SOUPS & STEWS

Ladle up...grab a bowl...soup's on! Contrary to popular belief, flavorful soups and stews can come together somewhat quickly. As a matter of fact, I find it to be a soothing solution to relieve some of the stress during these uncertain times. What economical, better and healthier way to take a brief respite from the chaotic lifestyle of today and nurture oneself in the privacy of a pot of soup or stew. Making a pot of savory soup or stew is a simple process and produces an enriched dish far beyond the powers of a can. Cooks who make their own soups and stews won't have it any other way and truly take pride in the end product. Try it just once, and you'll see what joy and comfort it brings on cold, wintry days in Hawai'i when curtains of rain and gusty winds blasts from the north.

This section features frequently requested recipes for soups and stews representing a number of ethnic groups that call Hawai'i home.

SOUPS

The smell of soup simmering symbolizes homecooking for many as somecan remember back in the day when homemakers routinely made soups from scratch with vegetables and herbs from neighborhood gardens and bones from the butcher which were only twenty-five cents or free.

Hot and Sour Soup

Yield: about 4 servings

This recipe is being shared with you in memory of a good friend, the late Robert Hsu, owner of the Maple Garden Restaurant in Moiliili. This dish was one of the specialties of the restaurant and Robert gave me the recipe when he did a cooking demonstration with me for the Chinese Narcissus Festival. Enjoy!

4 cups chicken broth
2 ounces lean pork or chicken, cut into strips
2 tablespoons bamboo shoots, julienne
1 tablespoon tofu, julienne
1 tablespoon black fungus, softened in water and julienne
2 tablespoons soy sauce
1 teaspoon black pepper
3 tablespoons cornstarch
3 tablespoons water
2 eggs, beaten lightly
2 tablespoons vinegar
1 tablespoon sesame oil
1 teaspoon minced green onion

Combine chicken broth with pork or chicken, bamboo shoots, tofu and black fungus in large saucepan; bring to a boil. Add soy sauce and pepper. Make paste of cornstarch and water; add to soup, making certain that it is mixed in evenly. Add eggs and vinegar to soup in a steady stream, stirring slightly as you add. Add sesame oil and green onion just before serving.

Beef Vegetable Soup

Yield: 4 to 6 servings

The Beef Vegetable Soup is hearty, healthy, and satisfying without the cream or butter roux used in many thick soups.

2½ pounds beef soup bone with meat
2 quarts water
1 tablespoon salt
¼ teaspoon fresh ground pepper
1 cup chopped onion
1 cup chopped celery
1 cup diced carrots
1 cup diced potatoes
1 can (10½ oz.) stewed tomatoes

Combine soup bone with water, salt and pepper in large pot; cover and bring to boil. Skim. Add onion and celery; bring to a boil again; lower heat and simmer, covered, until tender (2 to 3 hours). Remove meat from bone. Add meat and remaining ingredients to broth and cook, covered, 15 to 20 minutes or until vegetables are tender. Adjust seasoning as desired. Serve hot.

Portuguese Bean Soup

Yield: 6 to 8 servings

One of Hawai'i's comfort food is this ever-popular soup that's on the menu of many restaurants.

2 ham shanks
1 package (12 oz.) Portuguese sausage, cut into ½-inch pieces
1½ quarts water
1 can (8 oz.) tomato sauce
1 large onion, wedged
2 potatoes, cubed
1 carrot, cubed
1½ teaspoons salt
Dash of fresh ground pepper
2 cans (15 oz.) kidney beans, drained

Simmer ham shanks and Portuguese sausage in water for 2 hours. Add remaining ingredients; cook 15 to 20 minutes or until vegetables are done. Serve hot.

Oxtail Peanut Soup

Yield: about 4 servings

An all-time favorite among Islanders. There are many variations of this soup but this one was taught to me by a Chinese chef. You'll find this soup offered in many restaurants throughout the Islands as it is a meal in itself when served with hot steamed rice.

5 pounds oxtail, disjointed and fat removed
3 quarts water
1½ cups shelled raw peanuts
1 clove garlic, crushed (optional)
2 small pieces dried orange peel (kwo kee)
1 piece star anise
3 pieces dried mushrooms (shiitake), optional
1 piece (1-inch) fresh ginger root, crushed
¼ cup sherry or whiskey
2 teaspoons salt

Condiments:
Blanched Chinese cabbage, optional
Chopped green onion
Chinese parsley
Grated fresh ginger
Soy sauce

Parboil oxtail in enough water to cover for 10 minutes. Drain. Rinse once and add 3 quarts water. Add next 9 ingredients and simmer until oxtail is tender, about 2 to 3 hours. Garnish with Chinese cabbage, green onion and Chinese parsley accompanied by a dish of grated fresh ginger and soy sauce.

Jook

Chicken Rice Soup

Yield: 6 to 8 servings

Chicken bones
3 quarts water
1 cup rice, washed and drained
2 pieces dried mushrooms (shiitake), softened and slivered
½ chung choy (salted preserved cabbage), minced
1 ½ teaspoons salt
1 teaspoon sherry
Minced green onion
Chinese parsley (cilantro)

Place bones and water in large kettle; simmer 30 to 45 minutes. Add rice, mushrooms, chung choy and salt; simmer 45 to 60 minutes. Stir in sherry just before serving. Garnish with green onion and Chinese parsley to serve.

VARIATION:
Turkey Rice Soup: Substitute turkey wings or bones for chicken bones. Seved piping hot with a generous portion of cilantro, this soup is perfect for sharing family-style, in a cozy setting.

Kim Chee Soup

Yield: about 4 servings

When the weather turns chilly, huddle over a steaming bowl of warmth with hot Kim Chee Soup.

¼ pound lean pork, cut into small pieces
2 teaspoons slivered fresh ginger
3 cups water
1 potato, pared and cut into bite-sized pieces
1 carrot, pared and cubed
1 small daikon or turnip, cut into strips
½ cup kim chee, drained and chopped
1½ tablespoons red miso (soy bean paste)
¼ cup chopped green onion

Stir-fry pork with ginger in a nonstick saucepan. Add water and bring to a boil; simmer 2 to 3 minutes. Add potato, carrot and daikon or turnip; cook over low heat until vegetables are tender, about 10 minutes. Stir in kim chee and miso; simmer additional 1 to 2 minutes. Garnish with green onion to serve.

Miso Soup

Yield: 4 to 6 servings

A traditional Japanese soup that is truly a comfort food that can be varied in numerous ways.

6 cups water
½ cup dried shrimps
½ cup miso (soy bean paste)
1 tablespoon wakame (seaweed), soaked in water
½ block tofu, cut into cubes
¼ cup minced green onion

Cook shrimps in water for 20 minutes; strain. Add miso, wakame and tofu; cook 10 minutes over low heat or until tofu is heated through. Serve hot, garnished with green onion.

VARIATIONS:

• **Miso Soup With Egg:** Drop whole egg(s) into hot soup; bring to a boil; cook over low heat until egg is of desired doneness.

• **Mochi Miso Soup:** Add small mochi pieces to hot soup; cook over low heat until mochi is softened.

• **Miso Rice Soup:** Add cooked rice to miso soup; cook over low heat until rice is heated through.

Lentil Soup

Yield: 15 to 20 servings

8 cups vegetable stock or water
1 package (16 oz.) lentils, rinsed
2 bay leaves
1 medium onion, finely chopped
1 to 3 large ribs of celery with leaves,
    cut into ½-inch pieces
2 to 3 large carrots, cut into 1-inch
    chunks
2 zucchini, cut into 1-inch chunks
2 cloves garlic, mined
2 teaspoons minced fresh parlsey or
    dried
1 teaspoon dried thyme
1½ cups tomato juice
¼ cup red wine vinegar
1 teaspoon salt, or to taste
Pepper to taste
1 fresh red chili pepper, optional

In a large pot combine stock or water with lentils and bay leaves. Bring to a boil. Reduce heat to low, cover and simmer for about 30 minutes, or until lentils are just soft. Add onions, celery, carrots, zucchini, garlic, parsley, and thyme and cook additional 5 minutes. Add remaining ingredients. Cover and simmer 30 to 60 minutes, or until vegetables are tender.

STEWS

Both stews and soups are a combination of vegetables, meat or fish cooked in liquid with stew containing less liquid than soup. The cooking process differs too as some soups can be made quickly in as little as 20 minutes while stews always require more than an hour to simmer and stew.

Also stews are always served hot whereby soups may be served either hot or cold.

Beef Stew

Yield: 6 to 8 servings

2 pounds stewing beef, cut into 1-inch cubes
½ cup flour
¼ cup salad oil
2 medium onions, wedged
5 cups water, more as needed
2 bay leaves
2 teaspoons salt
¼ teaspoon pepper
2 8-oz. cans tomato sauce OR
  1# 13½-oz. can whole tomatoes
4 small carrots, cut into 1-inch pieces
4 small potatoes, pared and quartered
1 cup sliced celery

Dredge beef in flour; brown lightly on all sides in hot oil. Add onions and brown lightly. Add water and bay leaves; simmer 1½ hours or until beef is tender. Add remaining ingredients; simmer additional 30 to 45 minutes or until vegetables are done. Adjust seasoning, if needed.

VARIATION:
Add 2 cups round cabbage slices, if desired. My grandchildren love cabbage in stews.

Tinola

Filipino-Style Chicken Stew

Yield: 4 to 6 servings

1 clove garlic, minced
1 tablespoon salad oil
2½ pound frying chicken,
  cut into 1½-inch pieces
1 medium onion, diced
1 medium tomato, diced
1 tablespoon minced ginger
3 cups water
2½ teaspoons salt
4 cups (2 medium) very green papaya,
  pared, seeded and cut into ¾-inch
  cubes

Sauté garlic in salad oil until golden brown. Add chicken and cook for 5 minutes, stirring frequently. Add onion, tomato and ginger and cook an additional 4 to 5 minutes, stirring occasionally. Add water and seasonings. Cover and simmer 15 to 20 minutes. Add papaya and simmer for 5 to 10 minutes or until papaya begins to turn translucent. Serve hot.

TIPS:

• Very green papaya, when cut, should have no orange or pink color at all, and the seeds should be white.

• To make gravy, use 2 tablespoons each of drippings and flour for each cup of liquid.

Kari Kari

Filipino-Style Oxtail Stew

Yield: 8 servings

5 pounds oxtail pieces
5 tablespoons salad oil
1 tablespoon achiote seeds
1 onion, thinly sliced
2 cloves garlic, crushed
3 quarts water
1 tablespoon salt
½ cup rice
½ cup salted peanuts
1½ pounds long eggplants, cut in ½-inch
  lengths
1 pound long beans, cut in 2-inch lengths

In a large sauce pot, brown oxtail pieces in 3 tablespoons of the oil. Remove oxtail pieces; drain. Heat remaining 2 tablespoons oil with achiote seeds for 2 minutes; strain and discard seeds. Sauté onion and garlic in the achiote oil. Add oxtail pieces, 2 quarts of the water, and the salt; bring to a boil. Lower heat and simmer for 2½ hours; skim excess fat. In a small skillet, toast rice over low heat until rice is golden brown. Put rice info a blender; cover, and blend to a powder. Empty blender and put peanuts into blender; cover and blend until peanuts are finely ground. Add rice powder, ground peanuts, eggplants, beans, and the remaining 1 quart of water to the stew. Bring to a boil; lower heat and cook 15 more minutes.

Oven Braised Oxtail Stew

Yield: 8 to 10 servings

4 pounds oxtail, disjointed
1 cup flour
1 clove garlic, minced
¼ cup salad oil
6 cups water
2 bay leaves
1 tablespoon salt
¼ teaspoon pepper
1 8-ounce can tomato sauce
2 medium onions, wedged
4 medium carrots, quartered
4 medium potatoes, quartered
1 cup sliced celery

Dredge oxtail, in ½ cup flour. Brown oxtail and garlic in oil in uncovered Dutch oven at 400°F for 30 to 45 minutes; stir occasionally. Drain off excess oil. Add water and bay leaves. Cover and bake. Temperature: 325°F. Time: 3½ hours. Add remaining ingredients; cook additional 30 to 45 minutes or until, vegetables are tender. Make a smooth paste of remaining flour with water; add to stew to thicken, if desired.

Beef Curry Stew

Yield: 6 to 8 servings

This is the best local-style curry stew ever!

2 pounds stewing beef, cut into 1-inch cubes
2 tablespoons flour
2 tablespoons salad oil
2 large onions, wedged
1 clove garlic, minced (optional)
4 cups water
2 teaspoons salt
1 tablespoon curry powder
½ teaspoon pepper
4 small carrots, cut into 1-inch pieces
4 small potatoes, quartered
1 cup sliced celery
¼ cup flour
¼ cup water

Dredge beef in flour; brown lightly on all sides in hot oil. Add onion and garlic; brown lightly. Add water; cover and simmer 1½ hours or until beef is tender. Add seasonings and vegetables; cook additional 30 minutes or until vegetables are cooked. Make paste of flour and water; add to stew and cook until thickened.

NOTE: Add more salt and curry powder, if desired.

Taro Stew

Yield: 6 servings

¼ cup flour
½ teaspoon salt
Dash of pepper
2 pounds stew meat
2 tablespoons salad oil
1 onion, chopped
1 clove garlic, crushed
1 small piece ginger root, crushed
 2 Hawaiian red peppers, seeded and
  minced
½ teaspoon peppercorns
5 cups water
2 large carrots
2 pounds taro
1 cup chopped green onions
1 teaspoon Hawaiian salt
Poi to thicken, if desired

Combine flour, salt, and pepper. Dredge meal in flour mixture. In a large sauce pol, heal oil and brown meat. Stir in onion, garlic, ginger, peppers, and peppercorns. Add water; cover and simmer for 2 hours or until meat is tender. Cut carrots and taro into 1-inch pieces. Add to stew; cover and simmer for 30 to 40 minutes. Add green onions and salt just before serving. Thicken stew with poi if using.

Chicken Curry

Yield: 6 to 8 servings

This was a very popular entreé for many local dinners in Hawai'i. The condiments were often placed in coconut cups on the buffet whcih made for a very Hawaiian-style presentation.

1 3-pound stewing chicken, cooked,
  boned and cut in bite-size pieces
¾ cup onion, minced
1 clove garlic, minced
1 slice ginger, minced
2 tablespoons butter or margarine
1 tablespoon curry powder
2 tablespoons cornstarch
1 teaspoon salt
1 cup chicken broth
½ cup evaporated milk, undiluted
1½ cups coconut milk
½ teaspoon monosodium glutamate
  (MSG), optional
2 tablespoons sherry

Suggested Condiments:
Grated coconut, mango chutney, macadamia nuts, peanuts, chopped crisp fried bacon, and green onion

Sauté onion, garlic and ginger in butter or margarine. Blend in curry powder, cornstarch and salt. Stir in broth, evaporated and coconut milk, stirring constantly until thickened. Add chicken and reheat. Just before serving, add monosodium glutamate (if using) and sherry. Serve over steamed rice and top with condiments, as desired.

Tripe Stew

Yield: 6 servings

3 pounds honeycomb tripe, cleaned
2 teaspoons salt
2 slices bacon, chopped
2 cloves garlic, minced
2 tablespoons vinegar
1 large onion, chopped
2 cans (8 oz) tomato sauce
¼ cup minced parsley
1½ cups water
½ teaspoon pepper

Put tripe into large sauce pot; cover with water. Add salt; bring to a boil. Lower heat and simmer for 2 to 3 hours or until tender; drain. Cut tripe into 1½ x ¼-inch strips. Fry bacon in saucepot until crisp. Add tripe, garlic, vinegar, and onion; cook 5 minutes. Stir in remaining ingredients; cook 10 additional minutes.

EGGS 'N THINGS

According to East Indian history wild fowl were domesticated as early as 3200 BC. Egyptian and Chinese records show that fowl were laying eggs for man in 1400 BC and Europe has had domesticated hens since 600 BC. The incredible egg has been around for a long while!

Eggs are incredible for many reasons. They are all natural and packed with 13 essential vitamins and minerals, high quality protein, unsaturated fat and antioxidants— at total calories of only 70 calories. Eggs are among the healthiest, most nutritious foods on our planet and it also happens to be just about everyone's favorite food. Eggs are very versatile, and can be used in many different ways of preparation from hard boiled to microwave. It can also be used for dishes such as omelets to elegant souffles.

Cook Eggs Benedict for brunch, bake a Caramel Custard Flan for dessert or tasty Oyako Donburi (Egg-Chicken Rice Bowl) for a quick lunch or dinner. Whatever you choose to cook with the incredible egg will be enjoyed by all!

Tamago Meshi
Eggs & Rice

Yield: 2 to 3 servings

Nothing like breaking an egg into a bowl of hot, steaming rice! The egg cooks almost instantly upon contact with the hot rice and a nourishing dish that is homey and comforting. This was one of the first dishes my daughter, Shari, learned to prepare as a youngster.

2 large eggs
2 tablespoons shoyu
¼ cup minced green onion, optional
4 cups hot cooked rice
¼ cup cooked petite peas, optional

Combine first 3 ingredients and whisk eggs until frothy. Pour over hot rice; add peas and toss gently. Serve immediately.

Egg Foo Yong
Chinese Egg Omelette

Yield: 4 servings

4 eggs, well beaten
½ cup cooked pork, ham, chicken or shrimp, diced
2 cups bean sprouts, washed and drained
½ cup minced green onion
½ teaspoon cornstarch
¼ teaspoon salt
¼ teaspoon sugar
Dash of pepper
Dash of monosodium glutamate (MSG), optional

Sauce (optional):
1 cup chicken broth
¼ teaspoon salt
1 tablespoon cornstarch
2 teaspoons soy sauce
¼ teaspoon monosodium glutamate (MSG), optional

Combine eggs with next 8 ingredients. Pan fry egg mixture in hot oil using about 2 tablespoons for each omelette. Fry 2 to 3 minutes on each side or until egg is cooked.

To prepare sauce, combine ingredients and cook until thick, stirring constantly. Serve over Egg Foo Yong.

NOTE:
Bamboo shoots, water chestnuts, dried mushrooms and celery may be added. Stir-fry vegetables about 1 to 2 minutes; cook and add to egg mixture.

Omelet

Yield: 2 servings

1 tablespoon butter or margarine
3 eggs
3 tablespoons milk
¼ teaspoon salt
⅛ teaspoon black pepper

Place butter in an 8-inch round glass cake dish. Microwave 1 to 1½ minutes or until melted. Beat together remaining ingredients and pour into glass dish.

Microwave on ROAST-8, 2 minutes. Move cooked portion of egg to center of dish. Microwave on ROAST-8, 1½ minutes. Give dish a ½ turn. Microwave ½ to 1 minute on ROAST-8. Let stand 2 minutes before serving.

To serve, carefully loosen omelet from sides of dish with a rubber spatula. If desired, add filling, then fold omelet in half and serve.

VARIATION:

Western Omelet: Place 1 tablespoon butter or margarine in a 2-cup glass measuring cup. Microwave ½ minute. Stir in ¼ cup chopped ham, 2 tablespoons each chopped onion and green pepper. Cover with a paper towel and microwave 2 to 2½ minutes or until tender. Spoon over omelet and serve.

Eggs Florentine

Yield: 6 servings

2 pkg (10 oz size) frozen chopped spinach
6 eggs, poached
3 tablespoons butter or margarine
3 tablespoons flour
½ teaspoon salt
Dash of ground red pepper
1¼ cups milk
¼ cup heavy cream, whipped
¼ cup grated Parmesan cheese

Cook spinach according to package directions; drain. Put spinach in a 21 x 7 ½ x 2-inch broiler-safe baking dish. Make 6 depressions in the spinach and put one egg in each hollow. In a saucepan, melt butter; stir in flour, salt, and red pepper. Gradually add milk; cook, stirring constantly, until mixture thickens. Remove from heat and fold in whipped cream. Pour sauce over eggs and spinach; sprinkle with cheese. Broil 3 inches from unit in electric oven for 3 to 4 minutes, or until cheese is lightly browned.

Easy Hollandaise Sauce

Yield: ¼ cup

¾ cup butter or margarine
3 tablespoons lemon juice
4 egg yolks
¼ teaspoon salt

In a saucepan, melt butter over low heat until it bubbles, but not brown. Put remaining ingredients into blender; cover; set on high speed. Immediately remove feeder and slowly add butter in a steady stream. Continue blending until thickened. Serve over steamed vegetables or Eggs Benedict.

Eggs Benedict

Split, toast, and butter English muffins. Top each half with a slice of ham, Canadian bacon, or turkey bacon, poached egg, and a generous spoonful of Hollandaise Sauce. Sprinkle with paprika and garnish with parsley.

Super Easy Chawan Mushi

Yield: 6 servings

You must try this easy version of Chawan Mushi that includes many little bits of tasty treasures such as shiitake mushrooms, kamaboko, and shrimp hidden in the decorative cups of hot custard.

**1 can (10¾ oz.) condensed chicken
    noodle soup**
1 can water
4 eggs, beaten lightly

Mix soup, water, and eggs together. Pour into chawan mushi containers or custard cups. Gently steam on medium-low heat with the containers covered, for about 20 minutes. To serve, place container on a small saucer and add a small spoon.

**1 can (10¾ oz.) condensed chicken
    noodle soup**
**1 can of liquid, combination of water and
    liquid from soaking mushrooms**
4 eggs, beaten lightly
**6 small dried shiitake mushrooms,
    soaked and stems trimmed, (reserve
    the soaking liquid)**
6 slices of kamaboko or other fishcake
6 raw shrimp, shelled and deveined
6 sprigs of watercress or fresh spinach

Mix soup, water, mushroom liquid, and eggs. Place shiitake, and kamaboko into the chawan mushi containers or custard cups; pour in soup mixture to about ⅔ full. Place shrimp and sprig of watercress or spinach on lop. Cover and steam gently on medium low for 20 minutes. Serve on a saucer with a small spoon.

NOTE:

For those allergic to shrimps, use sliced kamaboko (steamed fishcake) or chikuwa (broiled fishcake).

Caramel Custard Flan

Yield: 8 to 10 servings

A sweet, smooth, thick custard that is perfectly flavored. I like it best when it's well chilled.

¾ cup granulated sugar
4 eggs
1 can (14-oz.) sweetened condensed milk
1 cup water
1 tablespoon rum, if desired
1 teaspoon vanilla extract

Place sugar in a heavy skillet. Heat over a medium flame setting until sugar melts and turns to a light golden color. Stir constantly during heating. Pour melted sugar into an 8-inch round cake pan, tilting to evenly coat bottom of pan. Set aside to cool while preparing custard. Beat eggs. Gradually beat in sweetened condensed milk then blend in remaining ingredients. Pour egg mixture over caramel-coated pan. Place round cake pan in a larger shallow pan. Fill larger pan with ½-inch of hot water. Bake at 350°F. for 35 to 40 minutes or until a silver knife inserted in center of flan comes out clean. Cool flan. Unmold by loosening flan from pan by running knife around edge of pan and inverting onto serving dish. Allow caramel syrup to run down sides of custard. Cut into wedges and serve.

Oyako Donburi
Rice with Chicken and Egg Topping

Yield: 4 to 6 servings

Donburi is a deep bowl with a lid used for "donburi-mono," which is hot cooked rice topped with meat, fish, egg or vegetables, drizzled with a sauce to flavor the rice. Mom frequently made this dish, as it is a typical Japanese "meal in one." Simply delicious!

1 pound boneless chicken, cut into thin slivers
4½ cups chicken broth
6 small bamboo shoots, slivered
1 medium round onion, cut into thin slices
2 teaspoons salt
2 teaspoons sugar
2 tablespoons shoyu
¼ cup mirin (sweet rice wine)
½ cup minced green onion
6 eggs, beaten

9 cups hot cooked rice

Toasted ajitsuke (flavored) nori, for garnish

Simmer chicken in broth for 5 minutes. Add next six ingredients; bring to a boil. Add green onion. Pour beaten egg over chicken mixture. Cover and cook over low heat for 30 seconds. Serve in individual bowls over hot rice. Garnish with crushed, toasted nori (seaweed), if desired.

Shirred Egg Soup

Kakitama Jiru

Yield: 4 to 8 servings

Simply good comforting soup anytime! Love it as a quick "pick-me-upper" when exhausted.

4 cups chicken broth
3 eggs, slightly beaten

Bring chicken broth to a boil, add beaten eggs slowly, stirring constantly. Garnish with sprigs of watercress, minced green onion, peas or a sliver of lemon rind to serve.

Portuguese Sausage Quiche

Yield: 6 to 8 servings

Outstanding luncheon dish—a must!

1 9-inch pastry with deep rim, unbaked
1 7-ounce package Portuguese sausage, chopped
1 small green pepper, chopped
2 cups Monterey Jack cheese, grated
4 eggs, beaten
1 cup half & half

Prick bottom of pastry and bake partially. Temperature: 400°F. Time: 10 minutes or until pale gold.

Sauté Portuguese sausage for 1 minute. Add green pepper and Sauté until soft. Spread evenly over bottom of partially baked pastry. Sprinkle cheese over top.

Beat eggs and half & half together. Pour over cheese. Bake. Temperature: 350°F. Time: 30 to 40 minutes or until knife inserted in center comes out clean. Let stand 10 minutes before slicing.

SAUCES

We rely on various sauces to flavor our food. A spectacular dish can't be cooked without an awesome sauce. A few hours devoted to shopping and simple cooking will give you a supply of homemade sauces infused with spices and flavorful ingredients. That in turn will launch dozens of recipes and weeks of great eating. One can certainly purchase a jar of commercial sauce but why bother when it takes only a few minutes to make your own for less—just the way you and your family like it!

Stir-Fry Sauces

Yield: about ⅓ cup sauce

Stir-frying is a great way to serve nutritional dishes relatively inexpensively as the expensive meats are extended with various vegetables. This is also a fast way to get dinner on the table.

Whisk together cornstarch with the second ingredient until well-blended then whisk in the remaining ingredients; pour into the stir-fry mixture, stirring well to coat evenly and cook until gravy thickens, about 15 seconds. Transfer the stir-fry dish to a bowl and serve immediately.

SESAME SOY SAUCE

1½ teaspoons cornstarch
2 teaspoons rice vinegar
⅓ cup chicken broth
2 tablespoons soy sauce
1 tablespoon sugar
1 tablespoon minced green onion
2 tablespoons toasted sesame seeds
2 teaspoons sesame oil
½ teaspoon minced garlic

CHINESE BLACK BEAN SAUCE

1½ teaspoons cornstarch
1½ teaspoons sherry
½ cup chicken broth
1½ tablespoons Chinese black bean/
   garlic sauce
1 tablespoon sugar
1 teaspoon Asian chili paste
½ teaspoon minced fresh ginger root

CANTONESE ORANGE OR LEMON SAUCE

1½ teaspoons cornstarch
2 teaspoons soy sauce
⅓ cup chicken broth
2 tablespoons orange or lemonade
   concentrate
2 tablespoons sherry
1½ teaspoons oyster sauce
1 teaspoon sugar
½ teaspoon minced fresh ginger

Suggested Stir-Fry Mixtures

- Chicken with shiitake mushrooms, broccoli, carrots and sugar snap peas with sesame soy sauce

- Pork with shiitake mushrooms, asparagus, red onions, carrots and bok choy with Chinese black bean sauce

- Shrimp with onion, bell pepper wedges, pineapple chunks and shiitake mushrooms with Cantonese orange or lemon sauce

Teriyaki Sauce

Yield: About 10 cups

Who doesn't like "teriyaki" in Hawai'i? This sauce is soy sauce based and is used to marinate or glaze beef, pork, chicken. This basic sauce may also be used to flavor some of the one-pot dishes, such as sukiyaki, or used to flavor simmered Japanese dishes.

3 cups soy sauce
4 cups water
1 cup mirin or sake
2 cups sugar
Fresh ginger to taste, smashed
4 cloves garlic to taste, smashed

Combine all ingredients in saucepan; bring to a boil over medium heat. Stir to dissolve sugar and store in covered jar in refrigerator until ready to use as marinade, dipping, basting, or cooking sauce for a variety of meats and dishes.

VARIATIONS:

- Teriyaki Beef: Marinate thin slices of beef in Teriyaki Sauce 30 to 60 minutes before broiling or pan-frying.

- Teriyaki Fish: Cook whole fish or fish fillets in Teriyaki Sauce. Fish may also be broiled using Teriyaki Sauce for basting or pan-fried with sauce poured over to serve.

- Teriyaki Pork: Marinate thin slices of lean pork in Teriyaki Sauce 30 to 60 minutes before broiling or pan-frying.

TIP:
For those who insist on having sake or mirin in their teriyaki sauce, add about 1 cup mirin or sake.

Spicy Barbecue Sauce

Yield: 2 cups

This sauce is easy to prepare and delicious with shredded roasted beef brisket or pork tenderloin...especially good for spicy barbecue sandwiches!

2 tablespoons canola oil
½ cup chopped onion
1 tablespoon minced garlic
1 teaspoon ground cumin
¼ teaspoon cayenne pepper
1 cup tomato ketchup
½ cup vinegar (malt vinegar preferred)
¼ cup soy sauce
¼ cup dark brown sugar, packed
2 tablespoons Worcestershire sauce
¼ teaspoon liquid smoke flavoring

Heat oil in medium saucepan and Sauté onion, garlic, cumin and pepper 3 to 4 minutes over medium heat. Stir In remaining Ingredients and simmer, stirring constantly, until slightly thickened, about 8 to 10 minutes.

Maple Barbecue Sauce

Yield: about 3 cups

Everyone enjoys a good barbecue of which the "secret ingredient" is the sauce. Here's one that you'll enjoy once your try it—it is one of my favorites as I enjoy the subtle flavor of maple and it has a little "kick" to it.

1⅓ cup ketchup
⅔ cup cider vinegar
½ cup maple syrup
½ cup canola or olive oil
1 tablespoon Dijon mustard
½ teaspoon garlic salt
1 teaspoon Worcestershire sauce
½ teaspoon chili powder
½ teaspoon cayenne*
Dash hot pepper sauce*

Combine all ingredients in a quart jar; stir to combine or cover and shake vigorously until well combined. Use as marinade or glaze for meats and poultry.

*Decrease or delete if you don't like a spicy sauce.

Korean Barbecue Sauce

Yield: about 1 quart

A "standard" sauce for Korean barbecued dishes such as Kalbi and Kun Koki. It may also be used as a marinade for chicken or pork.

2 cups soy sauce
1½ cups sugar
½ cup toasted sesame seeds
½ cup canola oil
¾ cup minced onion
½ cup minced green onion
2 cloves garlic, crushed
1 piece (½-inch) ginger, crushed
1 teaspoon fresh ground pepper
1 teaspoon sesame oil

Combine all ingredients in jar; cover and refrigerate. Shake well before using as marinade for meats and poultry.

Tartar Sauce

Yield: about 1 cup

Tartar Sauce is a must for Hawai`i's fried fish and seafood dishes...and easy to make.

1 cup mayonnaise
1 tablespoon minced onion
1 tablespoon minced sweet pickle
1 teaspoon minced green olives, optional

Combine all ingredients; mix thoroughly. Serve with seafood.

Brown Mushroom Sauce

Yield: about 14 cups

Hawai`i loves brown gravy poured over almost everything and this sauce can also be served as gravy over your favorite meat dishes and roasts.

3 tablespoons butter or margarine
1 can (2 oz.) mushroom stems and pieces, drained
3 tablespoons flour
¼ teaspoon salt
Dash of ground pepper
Few drops Worcestershire sauce
½ cup consommé or beef or chicken broth
½ cup water

Melt butter in saucepan over low heat; add mushrooms, flour and seasonings and brown; add consommé and water gradually while stirring constantly. Cook until thickened. Sauce may be thickened with more flour and additional seasonings may also be added as desired (i.e., garlic salt, marjoram powders and bay leaf).

Su for Sushi, Namasu

Seasoned Rice Vinegar

Yield: 1 quart

2 cups sugar
2 cups rice vinegar
2 tablespoons salt

Boil together and cool. Sprinkle over cooked hot rice and use for sushi of your choice.

Katsu Sauce

Cutlet Sauce

Yield: About 1 cup

⅓ cup tomato ketchup
¼ cup soy sauce
¼ cup sugar
1 ½ teaspoons Worcestershire sauce
Dash of pepper
Dash of ground red pepper

Combine all ingredients; mix well and serve with chicken katsu or any other fried cutlets.

Hekka/Sukiyaki Sauce

Yield: 4½ cups

2½ cups soy sauce
1½ cups sugar
½ cup mlrln

Combine Ingredients and mix well. Store In glass jar for use as seasoning for Sukiyaki or other Japanese one-pot dishes.

Tosa-Zu

Seasoned Vinegar Sauce

Yield: 2½ quarts

This sauce keeps for 6 to 7 months in the refrigerator and improves with age. If the sauce seems strong for your taste, dilute portions of it with a little dashi. Keep the sauce handy for "instant"' sunomono (vinegar flavored dishes). When used as a dressing for salads, add more dash/to the basic Tosa-Zu.

5 cups rice vinegar
3 cups dashi
1 cup mirin
1 cup soy sauce
1½ cups sugar

Combine all ingredients in a saucepan; bring to a boll. Cool and keep refrigerated in covered jar.

VEGETABLES & SIDES

Vegetables have come into their own in recent years as supermarkets, grocery stores and farmers' markets have an array of fresh, frozen and canned vegetables available year 'round. Creative cooks prepare delicious side dishes to accompany your meals utilizing fresh produce from farm to table.

Vegetables are important in our diets for the minerals and vitamins as well as energy and fiber they provide. This section offers you some tips on the selection, proper storage, preparation and cooking of fresh vegetables which can contribute to the minimum loss of nutrients from the vegetables. In addition, you will enjoy the recipes for some fast and easy side dishes.

Frozen vegetables should be cooked according to package directions. Commercially canned vegetables can be heated, undrained, until hot and then drained before serving.

Suggestions On Selection, Storage And Cooking Vegetables

SELECTION

- Purchase vegetables that are in season.
- Plan to use one dark-green or deep-yellow vegetable daily.
- Choose one or two vegetables each day that may be served raw.
- Select fresh and crisp vegetables; avoid those with damaged or decayed spots.
- Purchase or harvest only enough perishable vegetables for immediate use.

STORAGE

- Discard inedible portions of vegetables in order to prevent further spoilage and to save storage space. Wash, if necessary, and drain.
- Store vegetables that wilt or spoil easily in the refrigerator in moisture-proof bags or any tightly covered container or place them in the hydrator.
- Store eggplant, green peppers and tomatoes on a shelf in the refrigerator.
- Store lima beans, soybeans and peas in the pods in a covered container in the refrigerator.
- Store staple vegetables, such as dry onions and potatoes, in dry ventilated bins.

PREPARATION

- Use vegetables as soon as they are purchased or harvested, or refrigerate as directed under "Storage." Vitamin values begin to decrease as soon as vegetables are harvested.
- Scrape or pare vegetables that are to be cooked without skins very thinly.
- Shred or cut vegetables just before cooking or serving.
- Do not soak pared or cut vegetables in water; doing so results in the loss of water soluble vitamins and minerals.
- Do not discard the outer green leaves of lettuce and cabbage if they are of good quality as they are rich in minerals and vitamins.

COOKING

- Cook vegetables only long enough to soften them or to make them palatable. Do not overcook them.
- Never use baking soda to preserve the color of a vegetable nor to shorten the cooking time since baking soda destroys vitamins.
- Add salt at the beginning of the cooking period because it tends to reduce losses of vitamins and minerals.
- Cook vegetables in a covered pan in order to lessen the destruction of certain vitamins.
- Start vegetables in boiling water and heat the water to the boiling point again quickly.
- Use only a small amount of boiling water in the bottom of the saucepan. Add vegetables, cover and "steam."
- When cooking green leafy vegetables, use only the water that clings to the

leaves after washing, add fat, using 1 to 2 tablespoons of fat for each pound of raw vegetables and "steam."

- Serve the small amount of water that remains in the saucepan after the vegetable is cooked since it contains some of the water-soluble nutrients.

- Serve vegetables as soon as possible after they are cooked.

- Since refrigeration and reheating of cooked vegetables further destroy vitamins, try to avoid having leftovers; utilize any that you do have in salads whenever possible.

Vegetable dishes and other side dishes are great budget stretchers and you'll find they add great enjoyment and variety to your meal. If you want to add an elegant touch to a dinner party, try something as simple as a drizzle of Hollandaise Sauce over steamed broccoli.

Szechwan Eggplant

Yield: 4 to 6 servings

Eggplant cooked with hot garlic sauce, almost like the way the Chinese restaurants serve it, is certain to become one of your favorite dishes. It is easy to prepare too!

<u>Sauce:</u>
2 tablespoons soy sauce
2 teaspoons vinegar
2 teaspoons sugar
2 medium Hawaiian red peppers, seeded and minced
1 teaspoon minced fresh ginger
1 teaspoon minced garlic
1 teaspoon cornstarch

1 pound eggplant, pared and cut into 2-inch strips

¼ pound pork, cut into strips
1 cup canola oil

Combine sauce ingredients in a small mixing bowl; set aside.

Heat oil in wok or skillet; fry eggplant until soft; remove from oil and set aside. Pour out all but 2 teaspoons of the oil; stir-fry pork for 1 minute or until cooked; drain pork and pour oil out. Stir in eggplant and sauce mixture; cook 1 minute or until sauce comes to a boil, stirring gently. Serve immediately.

Kim Chee

Korean-style Pickled Cabbage

Yield: about 1 quart

Kim Chee is served with every Korean meal and is also used as flavoring for soups and rich dishes.

2 pounds Chinese cabbage
½ cup rock (Hawaiian) salt
1 quart water

<u>Seasonings:</u>
2 teaspoons minced red chili pepper
½ teaspoon minced garlic
½ teaspoon minced ginger root
½ teaspoon paprika
1 tablespoon sugar

Wash cabbage and cut into 1½-inch lengths. Dissolve rock salt in water. Soak cabbage 3 to 4 hours. Rinse and drain. Combine seasonings and add to cabbage, mixing thoroughly. Pack into quart jar. Cover loosely and let stand at room temperature 1 to 2 days. Chill before serving.

Tofu Burger

Yield: 4 to 6 servings

Protein rich tofu is combined with chopped mixed vegetables then formed into patties and pan-fried in hot oil for a hearty side dish.

1 block firm tofu
1 large onion, finely chopped
1 cup shredded carrots
4 dried mushrooms, soaked and finely
  chopped
2 tablespoons butter or margarine
½ cup finely chopped celery
1 egg
½ cup flour+ 1 tablespoon wheat germ
  (optional)
2 tablespoons oyster sauce
Canola oil for pan-frying

Place tofu in cheesecloth and squeeze out liquid. Sauté onion, carrots and mushrooms in butter until onion is very soft, about 8 minutes. Set aside to cool. Mix together celery, egg, flour mixture and oyster sauce. Stir in carrot mixture. Then stir in crumbled tofu and blend well. Shape into patties (mixture will be soft). Fry in hot oil until golden brown on both sides. Drain on absorbent paper towel. Serve hot.

Tofu Tempura
Fried Soy Bean Curd

Yield: About 2½ dozen

Chopped cooked shrimp and a variety of mixed vegetables are combined with tofu, then fried in hot oil to make this tasty appetizer or side dish.

1 large (1 pound) block firm tofu (soy
  bean curd), mashed and excess water
  pressed out
¼ cup cooked shrimp, chopped
½ cup minced carrots
⅓ cup minced green onions
¼ cup finely chopped roasted peanuts
⅓ cup gobo (burdock root), finely
  chopped
2 tablespoons sugar
1½ teaspoons salt
½ teaspoon monosodium glutamate
  (MSG), optional
3 eggs, beaten

Canola oil for deep fat frying

Combine tofu with all ingredients, except oil; mix well. Drop by spoonfuls into oil heated to 365°F and fry until golden brown. Drain on absorbent paper. Delicious served hot or at room temperature.

E-Z Mix-and-Match Divan Supreme

Yield: 4 to 6 servings

Fast and easy for the busy family—anything that be put together quickly and be ready to serve within 30 minutes is appreciated.

2 packages (8 oz. each) frozen asparagus spears, cooked and drained
About 2 cups sliced, cooked chicken (or 4 to 6 slices)
1 can (10½ oz.) condensed cream of chicken soup
¼ cup milk
¾ cup grated, processed American cheese

Arrange asparagus in greased, shallow 1½-quart casserole; top with sliced chicken. Add combined soup and milk. Sprinkle cheese on top. Bake. Temperature: 450°F. Time: about 20 minutes.

VARIATIONS: Use the following combinations; directions above.

VEGETABLE	MEAT OR SEAFOOD	SOUP
2 packages (9 oz. each) frozen green beans, cooked and drained	2 cans (7 oz. each) tuna rinsed and drained	1 can (10½ oz.) condensed cream of mushroom soup
2 packages (8 oz. each) frozen broccoli, cooked drained	About 2 cups sliced, cooked ham (or 4 to 6 slices) (about 1¼ inch thick)	1 can (10½ oz.) condensed cream and of celery soup
2 packages (8 oz. each) frozen asparagus, cooked and drained	2 cans (4½ oz. each) shrimp, rinsed and drained	1 can (10 oz.) condensed frozen shrimp soup, thawed

Chicken Chop Suey

Yield: 4 to 6 servings

A stir-fry dish that is simple to make and enjoyed by everyone. However, Chop Suey is not really a Chinese dish—it is all American. The historical rumor around is that its creation links to a 1896 banquet held in honor of a Chinese diplomat, Li Hongzhang, in New York City.

1 pound boneless chicken, sliced
¼ cup canola oil
1 round onion, sliced
1 cup carrots, cut in strips
½ cup celery, sliced diagonally
1 package (9 oz.) chop suey mix (bean sprouts, cabbage, carrots)
½ cup stock or water
1 cup Chinese peas or green beans, sliced

Marinade:
1 tablespoon cornstarch
½ teaspoon salt
Dash pepper
2 teaspoons sherry
1 tablespoon oyster sauce
1 tablespoon soy sauce
2 teaspoons Worcestershire sauce
2 cloves garlic, crushed
1 slice ginger, minced

Combine marinade ingredients; marinate chicken for 15 minutes. Heat 2 tablespoons oil in skillet or wok. Sauté onion, carrots, celery and cauliflower 1 minute. Remove. Heat 2 tablespoons oil and sauté chicken 30 seconds; add vegetables. Mix well. Add marinade and water; cook 1 minute. Stir in Chinese peas or green beans. Cook to heat peas, about 1 minute. Serve immediately.

TIPS:
- To blanch almonds, add boiling water to cover. Allow almonds to stand until skins are easily removed.
- Almonds slice or cut most readily when warm and moist, immediately after being blanched.

Mix-and-Match Wikiwiki Vegetables

Yield: 6 to 8 servings

1 can (10½ oz.) condensed cream of mushroom soup
⅓ cup milk
2 packages (10 oz. each) frozen peas, thawed
1 cup purchased French fried onion rings

Combine soup and milk. Place ½ of peas in a 1½-quart casserole, cover with half of soup mixture and half of onion rings; repeat layers. Bake, covered. Temperature: 400°F. Time: 25 minutes; uncover and bake 10 minutes longer.

VARIATIONS: Use the following combinations; directions above.		
SOUP	VEGETABLE	TOPPING
1 can (10¾ oz.) cheddar soup	2 packages (8 oz. each) frozen cauliflower, thawed	1 cup crushed potato chips
1 can (10½ oz.) condensed cream of chicken soup	2 packages (8 oz. each) frozen asparagus, thawed	1 cup slivered almonds
1 can (10½ oz.) condensed cream of celery soup	2 packages (10 oz. each) frozen carrots, thawed	1 cup chow mein noodles
1 can (10½ oz.) condensed cream of mushroom soup	2 packages (10 oz. each) broccoli, thawed	1 cup broken pecans

VEGETABLE COOKERY

Time given below is for cooking in ½-inch boiling water in covered saucepan or as indicated. These times are for cooking vegetables to a just tender stage and will give the greatest retention of color and nutritional value.

VEGETABLE	PREPARATION FOR COOKING	APPROXIMATE TOTAL COOKING TIME IN MINUTES
Artichoke, French	Cut stems close to leaves. Remove outside bottom leaves. Cut ¾ inch from top of leaves.	35 to 45
Asparagus	Remove lower stalk up to crispness. Scrub lightly. Leave whole or cut in pieces.	Whole: 10 to 20 Pieces: 5 to 15
Beans Green or Wax Lima	Remove strings. Cut lengthwise or crosswise. Shell	15 to 30 25 to 30
Beets	Leave whole with 1 inch of stem and root end or peel and slice thin or dice.	Whole: 30 to 45 Sliced or Diced: 15 to 25
Broccoli	Remove leaves and tough parts of stalk. Stand heads in salted water 5 minutes. Drain. Split large stalk or cut in 1-inch pieces.	10 to 20
Brussels Sprouts	Remove wilted leaves. Leave whole.	10 to 20
Cabbage, green	Shred or cut in eighths or quarters.	Quartered: 10 to 15 Shredded: 3 to 10
Carrots	Leave whole. Slice or cut lengthwise.	Whole: 15 to 30 Sliced: 10 to 25
Cauliflower	Remove leaves. Leave whole or separate. Stand in salted water 5 minutes. Drain.	Whole: 15 to 25 Flowerets: 8 to 15
Celery	Scrub with brush. Trim off root and blemishes. Dice.	15 to 18

VEGETABLE	PREPARATION FOR COOKING	APPROXIMATE TOTAL COOKING TIME IN MINUTES
Corn, on the cob	Husk. Remove silk. Cook in boiling water to cover.	5 to 15
Eggplant	Peel. Slice or dice.	10 to 20
Greens, all Beet Chard, Swiss Collard Kale Mustard Spinach Turnip	Discard wilted leaves and tough stems. Wash. Cook in water which clings to leaves.	5 to 15 10 to 20 10 to 50 15 to 25 20 to 30 3 to 10 10 to 30
Okra	Leave whole or cut in ½-inch pieces	10 to 20
Onions	Peel. Leave whole.	Medium: 20 to 35
Parsnips	Peel. Core. Leave whole or cut in quarters.	Whole: 20 to 40 Quartered: 10 to 20
Peas Green Black-eyed	Shell.	10 to 20
Crowder, cream	Shell.	60 to 120
Potatoes White, medium	Peel or cook in skin.	Whole: 25 to 40 Quartered: 20 to 25
Sweet, medium	Peel or cook in skin.	Whole: 25 to 55 Quartered: 15 to 25
Rutabaga	Peel. Slice or dice.	20 to 30
Squash Hubbard Yellow Zucchini	Cut in pieces. Leave whole or slice. Slice.	15 to 20 10 to 20 10 to 15
Turnips	Peel. Leave whole, slice or dice.	Whole: 20 to 30 Sliced or Diced: 10 to 20

LAST BITE

The last bite to any meal is dessert and the dessert you choose usually complements the meal—a light dessert like a strawberry parfait is perfect after a large meal while a molten chocolate cake will be enjoyed the most after a more moderate meal.

Desserts are also wonderful ways to celebrate special occasions—A Strawberry Cheesecake for Valentine's or Fluffy Key Lime Pie for an Aloha party.

Making desserts is about creating something special for loved ones...so, get out your mixer and start baking one of these easy-to-make scrumptious desserts!

CAKES & FROSTINGS

Just about everyone enjoys freshly baked, delicious frosted cakes. You'll love the mouth-watering variety of cake recipes that you'll find here plus they're easy to make.

Basic Chiffon Cake

Yield: 8 to 10 servings

Chiffon cakes are my favorite as they are light and airy.

2 eggs, separated
1½ cups sugar, divided
2¼ cups cake flour, sifted
1 tablespoon baking powder
1 teaspoon salt
⅓ cup salad oil
1 cup milk
1½ teaspoons vanilla

Beat egg whites until frothy. Gradually beat in ½ cup sugar. Continue beating until very stiff and glossy.

Sift together remaining sugar, flour, baking powder and salt. Add salad oil, half of milk, and vanilla. Beat 1 minute, medium speed on mixer or 150 strokes. Add remaining milk and egg yolks. Beat 1 minute more. Fold in meringue. Pour into two greased and floured 8-inch layer cake pans. Bake. Temperature: 350°F. Time: 35 minutes. Cool. Frost as desired.

Chocolate Pudding Cake

Serves 10 to 12

½ packages (18¼ oz. size) chocolate
  cake mix
½ cup chopped macadamia nuts
¼ cup cocoa
1 cup sugar
1 teaspoon vanilla
2¼ cups hot water

Mix cake according to package directions. Stir in nuts. Pour into greased 9 x 13 pan. Mix cocoa and sugar; add vanilla and hot water. Pour cocoa mixture over cake batter. Bake. Temperature: 350°F. Time: 40 minutes. Serve warm with sweetened whipped cream.

Butter Cake

Yield: 8 to 10 servings

Just about everyone enjoys freshly baked, lusciously frosted cakes.

1 cup butter or margarine, softened
1¾ cups sugar
1½ teaspoons vanilla
4 eggs
3 cups cake flour
4 teaspoons baking powder
⅛ teaspoon salt
1 cup milk

Cream butter or margarine and sugar until light and fluffy. Add vanilla. Add eggs, one at a time, beating well after each addition. Sift dry ingredients together. Add to creamed mixture alternately with milk, beginning and ending with dry ingredients. Pour batter into two greased and floured 9-inch cake pans. Bake. Temperature: 350°F. Time: 30 to 35 minutes. Cool and frost.

VARIATIONS:

- Spice Cake: Add 1 teaspoon cinnamon, ¼ teaspoon ground cloves and ¼ teaspoon nutmeg to dry ingredients.

- Poppy Seed Cake: Add ½ cup poppy seeds to cake batter.

- Chocolate Cake: Add 1 square melted unsweetened chocolate to batter.

- Lemon Cake: Add 1 teaspoon lemon extract instead of vanilla.

- Macadamia Cake: Fold in 1 cup chopped macadamia nuts to batter.

Sour Cream Almond Frosting

Yield: about 1½ cups

5 tablespoons butter or margarine, softened
3 cups confectioners' sugar, sifted
4 tablespoons sour cream
¼ teaspoon almond extract
Toasted almonds

Cream butter or margarine; gradually beat in sugar. Add sour cream and almond extract and beat until frosting is light and fluffy. If frosting is too thick, add milk, ½ teaspoon at a time, until of right spreading consistency. Spread between layers and on sides and top of cooled cake. Garnish top in flower-petal design with toasted almonds.

TIP:
To blanch almonds, add boiling water to cover. Allow almonds to stand until skins are easily removed.

Red Velvet Cake

Serves 8 to10

1 cup butter or margarine
1½ cups sugar
2 eggs
½ teaspoon salt
2 tablespoons cocoa
2½ cups cake flour
1¼ teaspoons baking soda
1 cup buttermilk
1 bottle (1 oz.) red food color

Cream butter and sugar until light and fluffy. Add eggs, one at a time, beating well after each addition. Sift dry ingredients together; add to butter mixture alternately with but termilk, beginning and ending with flour mixture. Pour batter into two 8- or 9-inch layer pans sprayed with oil. Bake. Temperature: 350°F. Time: 30 to 35 minutes or until wooden pick inserted in center comes out clean. Frost with Butter Cream Frosting.

Butter Cream Frosting

Yield: frosting for 8-inch layer cake

The classic frosting for any cake—Enjoy!

⅓ cup butter or margarine, softened
4 cups confectioners' sugar, sifted
1 egg yolk, beaten
1½ teaspoons vanilla
2 tablespoons evaporated milk

Cream butter and half the sugar, blending well. Add egg yolk and vanilla. Gradually blend in remaining sugar. Add enough milk to make of spreading consistency. Frost any cake of choice.

Mini Lava Chocolate Cakes

Yield: 6 servings

The Lava Cake is also known as Molten Chocolate Cake and it is an all-time favorite.

1 package (6 squares) bittersweet baking chocolate (Valrohna, Scharffen Berger preferred), break into pieces
¼ pound (½ cup) butter, cut into chunks
1½ cups confectioners' sugar
½ cup flour
3 whole eggs
3 egg yolks

Suggested Garnishes:
Sweetened whipped cream
Ice cream
6 fresh raspberries

Grease six 6-ounce ovenproof custard cups, ramekins or soufflé dishes. Place on baking sheet; set aside.

Microwave chocolate and butter in large microwaveable bowl on HIGH 1 minute or MEDIUM (50%) 2 minutes or until butter is melted. Stir with wire whisk until chocolate is completely melted. Add sugar and flour; mix well. Whisk in whole eggs and egg yolks; beat until well-blended. Divide batter evenly into prepared ovenproof dishes. Bake. Temperature: 425°F. Time: 10 to 14 minutes or until cakes are firm around the edges but still soft in the centers. Let stand 1 minute.

Run small knife around cakes to loosen. Invert cakes carefully onto dessert dishes. To serve, cut in half, if desired; garnish with additional powdered sugar lightly sprinkled, dollop of sweetened whipped cream or ice cream and topped with fresh raspberries. Serve warm.

FLAVOR VARIATIONS:

Prepare as directed. Add 1 teaspoon pure almond extract, orange extract, vanilla extract, raspberry extract or ground cinnamon.

TIP:

Batter can be prepared day before. Pour batter into prepared cups or dishes; cover with plastic wrap; refrigerate. Bring to room temperature when ready to serve, uncover and bake as directed.

Prune Cake

Yield: 8 to 10 servings

There was a time when small pieces of this cake were used as the "groom's cake" and given as favors at weddings.

1 cup sugar
1 cup butter or margarine, softened
2 eggs
1 teaspoon vanilla
1 cup prune pulp
1½ cups cake flour
1½ teaspoons baking soda
1 teaspoon cinnamon
½ teaspoon ground cloves
½ teaspoon salt
½ cup sour milk
½ cup macadamia nuts, chopped

Cream sugar and butter or margarine until light and fluffy. Add eggs, one at a time, beating well after each addition. Beat in prune pulp.

Sift together flour, soda, cinnamon, cloves and salt. Add dry ingredients and sour milk alternately, beginning and ending with dry ingredients. Stir in nuts.

Pour into 2 greased 9-inch layer pans or a 9-inch tube pan. Bake. Temperature: 350°F. Time: 30 to 35 minutes (9-inch layers) or 1 hour (tube pan). Frost with Prune Frosting.

Prune Frosting

Yield: about 1½ cups

½ cup butter or margarine, softened
3 cups confectioners' sugar, sifted
3 tablespoons milk
½ cup minced, stewed prunes
½ teaspoon lemon extract

Cream butter or margarine and sugar until light and fluffy. Add milk, prune pulp and lemon extract; continue beating until mixture is well-blended and fluffy. Frost Prune Cake.

TIPS:

- Grated and ground nuts should not be used interchangeably. Grated nuts are fluffy and dry. They are sometimes used in place of flour in cookies and cakes. Ground nuts are more oily and compact.

- All-purpose flour can be substituted for sifted cake flour. Use 2 tablespoons less than 1 cup of sifted all-purpose flour when a recipe calls for 1 cup of sifted cake flour. Do not add cornstarch. This will result in a dry cake.

Strawberry Cheesecake

Yield: 12 to 16 servings

With this dessert, there is the rich flavor of cream cheese without all the calories as it uses only eight ounces of cheese.

Crust:
½ package zwieback or 16 graham crackers
¼ cup sugar
¼ cup butter or margarine

Filling:
1 package (8 oz.) cream cheese, softened
2 eggs
½ cup sugar
1 tablespoon lemon juice

Topping:
1 package (10 oz.) fresh frozen strawberries
3 tablespoons cornstarch

To prepare crust, roll zwieback or crackers into crumbs. Add sugar and butter and mix thoroughly. Press into bottom of 8-inch baking pan. Refrigerate.

To prepare filling, beat cream cheese until fluffy. Add eggs and continue beating until well-blended. Add sugar and lemon juice; beat to mix thoroughly. Pour filling into chilled crumb crust lined pan. Bake at 375°F. Time: 20 minutes. Cool and top with strawberry topping.

To prepare topping, drain strawberries and save liquid. Add strawberry liquid to cornstarch to make a smooth paste. Add remaining liquid and bring to boil, stirring constantly. Cook until thick, about 3 to 5 minutes. Add strawberries. Cool and spread over cheesecake.

Tropical Carrot Cake

Serves about 16

3 cups flour
2 teaspoons baking soda
2 teaspoons cinnamon
½ teaspoon salt
2 cups sugar
1½ cups canola oil
2 cups finely grated carrots
1 can (8¼ oz.) crushed pineapple
2 teaspoons vanilla
1½ cups chopped macadamia nuts
3 eggs

Spray 10-inch tube pan with oil; flour pan; set aside. Sift together flour, baking soda, cinnamon, and salt. Combine sugar and oil in large bowl of mixer. Add half of the flour mixture and mix well. Beat in carrots, pineapple, vanilla, and nuts. Add remain ing flour mixture; beat well. Add eggs, one at a time, beating well after each addition. Pour into prepared pan. Bake. Temperature: 350°F. Time: 60 to 70 minutes or until wooden pick inserted in cake comes out clean.

Liliko'i Spice Cake

Yield: 8 servings

Liliko'i is the Hawaiian name given to passion fruit and is one of the most popular locally grown fruits in Hawai'i. It has a pleasant texture and its citrus-like flavor is unsurpassed.

3 cups cake flour
1 teaspoon cinnamon
1 teaspoon ground cloves
½ teaspoon allspice
2 teaspoons baking powder
1 teaspoon baking soda
1 cup butter or margarine, softened
2 cups sugar
4 egg yolks
½ cup liliko'i (passion fruit) concentrate
½ cup water
4 egg whites

Sift together into a medium bowl cake flour, cinnamon, cloves, allspice, baking powder and baking soda; set aside. Thoroughly cream butter or margarine with sugar until light and fluffy. Add egg yolks, one at a time, beating well after each addition. Add flour mixture alternately with liliko'i concentrate and water, starting and ending with flour.

Beat egg whites until stiff but not dry. Fold batter into the beaten egg whites. Pour into two 9-inch greased cake pans. Bake. Temperature: 350°F. Time: 35 to 40 minutes. Frost with Liliko'i Fluff Frosting.

Liliko'i Fluff Frosting

Yield: Frosts 8-inch layer cake

2 egg whites
1 cup sugar
¼ teaspoon salt
⅓ cup liliko'i (passion fruit) concentrate
⅓ cup water

Combine ingredients in a large saucepan. Beat mixture 1 minute with mixer. Cook, beating constantly, until frosting forms stiff peaks, about 7 to 10 minutes.

Magical Cake Mixes

Cake mixes can save both time and money—especially when they're on sale. Follow package directions carefully and you can add your own individual touches.

- Poppy Seed Pound Cake: **Prepare 1 package pound cake mix according to package directions, adding ¼ cup oil with liquid. Add 3 tablespoons toasted poppy seeds and 1 teaspoon lemon extract ½ minute before end of beating time.**

- Coffee Spice Cake: **To 1 package (19.1 oz.) spice cake mix, add 4 teaspoons instant coffee to dry mix and add ¼ cup canola oil with other liquids**

- Strawberry Cake: **Add 1 package (3 oz.) strawberry gelatin to 1 package (19.1 oz.) white cake mix. Add ½ cup thawed, frozen strawberries and liquid, ¼ cup oil, 1 cup water and 4 eggs; Beat well. Pour into 3 greased and floured 9-inch pans. Bake. Temperature: 350°F. Time: 30 minutes.**

TIPS:
- When you have leftover egg yolks or egg whites, remember: 1 egg yolk equals about 1 tablespoon. 1 egg white equals about 2 tablespoons.

- To change from one pan size to another (when baking a cake, for example): Fill the pan usually used for the recipe with water to the proper level. Pour the water into the new pan to determine whether it is adequate. Remember that a change in pan size may also require a change in baking time and/or temperature.

- For accurate measurements, use a set of graduated measuring cups for measuring all dry ingredients. Use a glass measuring cup for liquid ingredients only.

Pineapple Upside Down Cake

Yield: About 20 to 24 servings

Upside-down cakes date to a time before reliable ovens, when cakes were often cooked on the stovetop, usually in a cast-iron skillet. Butter and sugar were caramelized in the bottom of the skillet, and the batter went on top. When the cake was inverted—voila! a cake with a golden glaze on top. Fruits and nuts were normally part of the glaze. Hawai'i's part in this comes through the Hawaiian Pineapple Co. (later Dole Foods), which popularized the pineapple version of the cake by publishing the recipe in magazine ads as a way to help sell its Hawaiian pineapple. The pineapple version is the modern standard for upside-down cakes.

½ cup butter or margarine
1½ cups brown sugar, packed
1 can (1 pound 4 oz.) sliced pineapple, drained
10 maraschino cherries
1 package (18.5 oz.) yellow cake mix

Melt butter or margarine in 13 x 9 x 2-inch pan. Stir in brown sugar and spread evenly in pan. Arrange pineapple slices on sugar mixture; place cherries in center of pineapple slices.

Prepare cake according to package directions. Pour batter over fruit, spreading evenly. Bake at 350°F oven for 35 to 40 minutes or until golden brown and wooden pick inserted in cake comes our clean. Cool slightly; invert onto a serving platter.

TIP:
Serve warm cake slices topped with ice cream, whipped cream, fruit, sour cream, yogurt, or your favorite sauce or pudding.

COOKIES

Let's always keep the cookie jar filled with classic favorites as Snickerdoodles, Chinese Almond Cookies, Chocolate Crinkles and more!

Chinese Almond Cookies

Yield: about 6 dozen

This recipe has stood the test of time. It is a basic recipe for Almond Cookies that I've been using for more than 50 years!

2 cups flour
1 cup sugar
½ teaspoon baking powder
½ teaspoon salt
⅔ cup shortening
1 egg, beaten
2 teaspoons almond extract
Red food coloring

Sift together flour, sugar, baking powder and salt. Cut or rub in shortening until mixture resembles fine cornmeal. Mix egg and almond extract; add to flour mixture. Mix well and knead gently for ½ minute. Form into balls the size of walnuts. Place on ungreased cookie sheet. Dip chopstick in red food coloring and make an indentation in the center of each cookie. Bake. Temperature: 325°F. Time: 20 minutes. Cool; store in airtight container.

Cornflake Cookies

Yield: About 3 dozen

These cookies are very easy to make and my grandchildren love to help me bake them. They especially love to roll the dough in the crispy cereal before baking.

1 cup butter or margarine, softened
¾ cup sugar
2 teaspoons vanilla extract
2 cups flour
3 cups (or more) cornflakes

Cream butter or margarine with sugar until light and fluffy; gradually add vanilla and flour; mix well. Form dough into large marble-size pieces and roll in bowl of crushed cornflakes. Place on ungreased baking sheets; flatten slightly using the bottom of a glass dipped in flour. Bake. Temperature: 350°F. Time: 10 to 15 minutes until golden yellow but not brown. Cool. Store in airtight container.

VARIATION:
Macadamia Nut Cookies: Stir in ½ cup chopped macadamia nuts to dough. Bake as directed until golden brown.

Wikiwiki Cookies

Yield: about 5 dozen

No other cookie recipe can be simpler than this—try it!

1 box (18 oz.) white or yellow cake mix
2 eggs
6 tablespoons melted butter

Combine ingredients and mix well. Drop by spoonfuls on ungreased cookie sheet. Bake. Temperature: 375°F. Time: 12 to 15 minutes. Cool; store in airtight container.

VARIATIONS:
- Maple Nut Cookies: Add 1 teaspoon maple extract and 1 cup nuts.
- Lemon Coconut Cookies: Add 1 teaspoon lemon extract and 1 cup coconut flakes.
- Chocolate Drop Cookies: Add 1 teaspoon vanilla extract, 1 cup chocolate chips and ½ cup chopped nuts.
- Raisin Drop Cookies: Add 1 teaspoon vanilla extract and 1 cup raisins.

TIP:
Most cookies are rich enough so that a greased cookie sheet is not necessary. If a cookie that does not require a greased cookie sheet is baked on a greased one, the cookie is likely to spread while baking and will have a deep brown, rather unattractive edge.

Energy Bars

Yield: 23 bars

Youngsters love to snack on these energy bars between meals. They store well in airtight jars for at least a week.

2½ cups crisp rice cereal
1 cup quick oats
¾ cups sunflower or sesame seeds
1 package (10 oz.) marshmallows
½ cup peanut butter
¼ cup (½ block) butter
¼ cup unsalted peanuts
½ cup raisins

Grease a 13 x 9-inch pan; set aside. Combine rice cereal, oats and sunflower or sesame seeds in saucepan; toast over medium heat for a few minutes. In a large saucepan, combine marshmallows, peanut butter and butter; melt over low heat. Stir in cereal mixture, peanuts and raisins; spread evenly into 9 x 13-inch pan; press firmly into prepared pan. Cool; cut into bars and wrap individually in waxed paper.

VARIATIONS:
- Cranberry Energy Bars: Substitute dried cranberries for raisins.
- Apricot Energy Bars: Substitute chopped, dried apricots for raisins.

Chocolate Crinkles

Yield: About 6 dozen

The tops of these cookies puff up and crack, making an attractive dark and white contrast...an interesting addition to the cookie tray year-round.

2 cups sugar
½ cup canola oil
2 teaspoons vanilla extract
4 (1-ounce) squares unsweetened baking chocolate, melted and cooled
4 large eggs
2 cups flour
2 teaspoons baking powder
½ teaspoon salt
½ cup powdered sugar, sifted

Mix together sugar, oil, vanilla, and chocolate in large bowl. Mix in eggs, one at a time, beating well after each addition. Stir in flour, baking powder, and salt; mix well. Cover and refrigerate, at least 2 to 3 hours. Roll chilled dough into 1-inch balls; roll in powdered sugar. Place about 2 inches apart on lightly greased baking sheet. Bake. Temperature: 350°F. Time: 10 to 12 minutes, or until no indentation remains when touched. Cool. If desired, sprinkle with additional powdered sugar when cooled.

Shortbread Cookies

Yield: about 3 dozen

I can never get enough of Shortbread Cookies. It just melts in your mouth and is simply delicious with a glass of milk or hot coffee! Have you had them dipped in chocolate? Yum!

2 cups butter or margarine, softened
1 cup sugar
4 cups flour
2 teaspoons vanilla

Cream butter or margarine and sugar until light and fluffy. Add flour and vanilla; mix well. Either use dough immediately by putting it through a cookie press onto ungreased cookie sheets, or chill overnight. To chill, shape dough into 2 oval rolls, about 2 inches across; wrap in waxed paper. The next day, slice dough into ¼-inch slices; place on ungreased cookie sheets. Bake. Temperature: 325°F. Time: 25 minutes.

Coconut Washboards

Yield: About 20 cookies

A popular cookie in the 1920s and 1930s and still popular today in some areas of the country, "washboards" got their name from the ridges made by pressing a fork into the dough before baking.

½ cup unsalted butter, softened
1 cup light brown sugar, firmly packed
1 teaspoon vanilla
¼ teaspoon coconut extract
1 large whole egg
1 large egg yolk
2 cups unbleached flour
¾ teaspoon double-acting baking powder
¼ teaspoon baking soda
Pinch of salt
1 cup sweetened coconut flakes, packed

In a bowl cream together butter and brown sugar until light; beat in vanilla, coconut extract, whole egg, and egg yolk. In another bowl, sift together flour, baking powder, baking soda, and salt. Stir the flour mixture into the butter mixture; stir in the coconut; cover and chill the dough for 20 minutes or until firm.

Spoon slightly rounded tablespoons of dough into floured palm of hand and form into 2½ inch long logs. Place logs 3 inches apart on greased baking sheets. Using a fork dipped in flour, press the back of the tines lengthwise into the logs, flattening them to 4 inches long and 1½ inches wide. (The marks from the tines of the fork should all be lengthwise.) Bake at 375°F for 10 to 12 minutes or until they are golden around the edges. Cool on baking sheets for 5 minutes then transfer the cookies to racks and cool completely.

Buttery Hawaiian Lemon Bars

Yield: About 24 bars

These luscious bars will remind you of Lemon Meringue Pie with a cookie crust.

Crust:
1 cup butter or margarine, softened
½ cup powdered sugar
2¼ cups flour

Filling:
4 eggs
2 cups sugar
1 teaspoons lemon zest
½ cup fresh lemon juice
½ cup flour
1 teaspoon baking powder
¼ teaspoon salt
Powdered sugar

To prepare Crust, beat butter and powdered sugar together in large mixer bowl until creamy; beat in flour, blending thoroughly. Spread mixture evenly over bottom of well-greased 9 x 13 x 2-inch baking pan. Bake. Temperature: 350°F. Time: 18 to 20 minutes or until light golden brown.

Prepare Filling by beating eggs in small mixer bowl until light. Gradually add sugar, beating until mixture thickens and turns lemon-colored. Add lenion zest, lemon juice, flour, baking powder, and salt; beat until smooth and well combined. Pour Filling mixture over baked crust and return to oven; bake additional 15 to 20 minutes or until topping is light golden brown. Place on rack to cool; sprinkle with sifted powdered sugar while still warm over top. Cool. Cut into bars to serve. Store in airtight container.

Favorite Brownies

Yield: about 16 to 20 bars

I can't imagine a collection of recipes without one or more brownie recipes so here are some of my favorites.

⅓ cup butter or margarine
1 (1-ounce) square unsweetened chocolate
1 cup sugar
¾ cup flour
½ teaspoon salt
½ teaspoon baking powder
2 eggs, slightly beaten
1 teaspoon vanilla extract
1 cup chopped nuts
Powdered sugar, optional

Melt butter or margarine and chocolate in 2-quart saucepan; remove from heat and stir in sugar. Sift together flour, salt, and baking powder; add to chocolate mixture. Beat in eggs. Stir in vanilla and nuts. Pour batter into greased 8- or 9-inch square cake pan. Bake. Temperature: 350°F. Time: 20 to 30 minutes. For extra chewy brownies use 8-inch pan and less baking time. For cakey brownies, use 9-inch pan and longer baking time. Cool and cut into bars. Sprinkle with powdered sugar, if desired.

VARIATIONS:

- Chocolate Chip Brownies: Add 1 cup chocolate chips to Favorite Brownie batter. Proceed as directed above.

- Chocolate Kisses Brownies: Cut brownies into approximately 1½-inch squares and press an unwrapped chocolate kiss candy on top while warm. Yield: About 25.

- Mac Nut Brownies: Add 1 cup chopped nuts to Favorite Brownie batter. Proceed as directed above.

SCRUMPTIOUS PIES

My family loves pies from delicious fruit pies with flaky crusts to the pat-in-the-pan crust that requires no rolling. You'll especially love the Custard Pie ala Hawai'i—soooo ono! You'll also love the Two-Crust Banana Pie other types of pies you can make.

Custard Pie

Yield: 1 (9-inch) pie

Due to shortages of fresh milk during the Second World War, Hawai'i bakers began to substitute evaporated milk in their recipes. The taste caught on in Island homes. If you're looking to give your custard desserts a distinctive local flavor, I recommend the use of evaporated milk.

5 eggs, slightly beaten
¾ cup sugar
½ teaspoon salt
¼ teaspoon nutmeg
3 cups undiluted evaporated milk
1 teaspoon vanilla extract
9-inch unbaked pie shell

Beat eggs slightly; stir in sugar, salt, nutmeg, milk and vanilla extract. Whisk to blend ingredients well. Pour into pie shell. Bake at 425°F for 30 to 40 minutes, or until knife inserted in center of pie comes out clean.

EASY PIE SHELLS

NAME	MAIN INGREDIENTS	SWEETENING	BUTTER	TIME AND TEMP
Graham Cracker, 9-inch pie	1⅓ cups crumbs	2 tablespoons sugar	⅓ cup melted	375°F, 8 minutes
Cookie, 9-inch pie: Vanilla or Chocolate or Gingersnaps	1½ cups crumbs	None	¼ cup melted	375°F, 8 minutes
Coconut, 9-inch pie	2 cups flaked coconut	None	¼ cup melted	300°F, 35 minutes
Zwieback, 9-inch pie	12/3 cups crumbs	3 Tbsp. sugar ½ teaspoon cinnamon	⅓ cup melted	400°F, 8 minutes
Chocolate Cereal, 9-inch pie	1½ cups rice cereal ¼ cup pecan halves	½ cup (3 oz.) semi-sweet chocolate bits, melted	2 tablespoons melted	Chill until firm

Combine ingredients. Reserve 2 to 3 tablespoons of mixture for topping, if desired (omit for Chocolate Cereal Crust). Press remainder on bottom and side of a greased pie pan (9 x 1½ inch). Bake in a preheated oven according to chart. Cool thoroughly.

Fluffy Key lime pie

Yield: 6 to 8 servings

Key lime pies were traditionally made with the juice of Key limes which are small limes grown in the Florida Keys; however, the juice of any lime works just fine. You'll enjoy this fluffy version of that infamous pie.

1 baked 9-inch pie crust
1 envelope unflavored gelatin
1 cup sugar
½ cup fresh lime juice
¼ cup water
4 eggs, separated
1 teaspoon zest of lime
1 drop green food color
1 cup whipping cream
Sweetened whipped cream for garnish, if desired

Combine gelatin, ½ cup of the sugar, lime juice, water and egg yolks in 1-quart saucepan. Cook over medium heat 5 to 7 minutes, stirring constantly, until mixture comes to a boil and thickens slightly. Remove from heat; stir in lime zest and food color. Pour mixture into large bowl; refrigerate until mixture begins to mound slightly, about 30 to 45 minutes.

In large bowl, beat egg whites until frothy and soft peaks form. Gradually add remaining ½ cup sugar, beating until stiff peaks form. In small bowl, beat whipping cream until stiff peaks form. Fold egg white and whipped cream into cooled lime mixture. Spoon into cooled baked shell. Refrigerate until firm, about 2 to 3 hours. Top with sweetened whipped cream to serve, if desired.

Stir 'N Pat Pastry

No other pie crust is easier to make than this. You'll love it!

2 cups flour
1 teaspoon salt
½ cup salad oil
¼ cup cold water or milk

Stir together flour and salt. Pour salad oil and cold water or milk into measuring cup (do not stir). Add all at once to the flour mixture. Stir lightly with fork; gather pastry into a ball. Press in bottom and up side of pie plate; flute. Fill and bake as directed in recipe or prick bottom and side with fork and bake. Temperature 475°F. Time: 10 to 12 minutes or until light brown; cool and fill as desired.

Pumpkin Chiffon Pie

Yield: 6 to 8 servings

Rather than the traditional pumpkin pie, here is a recipe for a "lighter" version of pumpkin pie that many people told me is better than the traditional one.

1 envelope unflavored gelatin
¼ cup water
3 eggs, separated
⅓ cup sugar
1¼ cups canned pumpkin
½ cup milk
½ teaspoon salt
1 teaspoon cinnamon
¼ teaspoon ground ginger
½ teaspoon allspice
¼ teaspoon nutmeg
¼ cup confectioners' sugar
9-inch crumb crust

Add gelatin to cold water; set aside to soften. Beat egg yolks slightly; add sugar and beat until blended. Add pumpkin, milk, salt, cinnamon, ginger, allspice and nutmeg. Mix; cook over medium heat, stirring constantly, until mixture comes to a boil. Cook 2 minutes. Add softened gelatin and stir until dissolved. Cool.

Beat egg whites until frothy. Add confectioners' sugar; beat until stiff peaks form. Fold meringue into pumpkin mixture. Pour into crust. Chill until set, about 1 hour. Top with sweetened whipped cream or whipped dessert topping, if desired.

> TIP:
> Condensed and evaporated milk should not be used interchangeably. Condensed milk is sweet and thick. Evaporated milk is ordinary milk from which about half the water has been removed; it has a consistency similar to cream. Nothing is more refreshing and scrumptious for dessert than fresh fruit!

Fresh Strawberry Pie

Yield: a 9-inch pie

Yum! Bright red, plump and juice vine-ripened strawberries fill the flaky shell. Topped with sweetened whipped cream, it's a scrumptious sight to behold!

1 9-Inch pie shell (see page 186)
1 cup sugar
3 tablespoons cornstarch
½ teaspoon salt
3 tablespoons white corn syrup
1 cup water
3 tablespoons strawberry-flavored
   gelatin
About 1 quart fresh strawberries,
   washed, and hulled
Sweetened whipped cream

Prick pie shell with a fork. Bake. Temperature: 450°F. Time: 12 minutes or until light brown. Set aside to cool.

Combine sugar, cornstarch, salt, syrup and water in saucepan; stir and cook over low heat until mixture thickens, about 5 minutes. Add gelatin and blend. Cool. Put berries into cooled, baked pie shell. Spoon gelatin mixture between berries. Chill thoroughly. Serve with sweetened whipped cream.

VARIATIONS:
- **Fresh Raspberry Pie:** Follow the recipe for Fresh Strawberry Pie except 1) substitute 1 quart raspberries for strawberries 2) substitute 3 tablespoons raspberry gelatin for strawberry gelatin 3) and decrease sugar to ¾ cup.

- **Fresh Blueberry Pie:** Follow the recipe for Fresh Strawberry Pie except 1) substitute 1 quart blueberries for strawberries 2) substitute 3 tablespoons lemon gelatin for strawberry gelatin 3) decrease sugar to ¾ cup and 4) add 2 tablespoons fresh lemon juice.

- **Fresh Peach Pie:** Follow the recipe for Fresh Strawberry Pie except 1) substitute 1 quart sliced, fresh peaches for strawberries 2) substitute 3 tablespoons peach gelatin for strawberry gelatin and 3) add 1 to 2 tablespoons lemon juice.

Coconut Cream Pie

Yield: 8 to 10 servings

This pie is very popular at most Hawaiian lūʻaus and local restaurants.

2 cups milk
½ cup sugar
¼ cup grated fresh coconut
5 tablespoons cornstarch
4 egg yolks
1 tablespoon butter
Pinch of salt
Vanilla extract to taste
1 (9-inch) baked pie shell

Meringue:
4 to 6 egg whites
Approximately 1 tablespoon sugar for each egg white
Grated fresh coconut

Put milk, sugar, salt, and coconut in saucepan over medium heat and cook until it comes to near boil; mix cornstarch and egg yolks together with a little water and add to milk mixture, stirring continually until thickened over low heat; add butter, salt and vanilla. Stir, cool and pour into baked and cooled pie shell. Top with meringue.

To prepare meringue, beat egg whites until stiff but not dry; add sugar gradually, beating continuously. Spread over cooled filling, sealing to edges of pastry. Sprinkle coconut over top. Brown in 400°F oven.

Guava Chiffon Pie

Yield: 8 to 10 servings

9-inch baked pastry shell

1 envelope unflavored gelatin
¼ cup water
4 eggs, separated
¼ cup lemon juice
3 tablespoons sugar
1 can (6 oz.) frozen guava juice, thawed
½ teaspoon cream of tartar
½ cup sugar
2 cups whipped cream or nondairy whipped topping

Soften gelatin in water; set aside. Beat egg yolks; beat in lemon juice and 2 tablespoons sugar; cook over low heat, stirring constantly until mixture is thickened. Stir in softened gela tin and remove from heat. Cool; stir in guava juice and chill until mixture begins to thicken.

Beat egg whites together with cream of tartar until soft peaks form; gradually add remaining sugar, beating until stiff. Fold in thickened guava mixture; pour into pie shell and chill until firm, about 3 hours. Serve with whipped cream or topping.

Caramel Apple Tarts

Yield: 6 to 8 servings

TIP:
Purchased refrigerated pie crusts may be substituted with homemade crust (see page 186)

There is no rule that says you need to start from scratch to prepare great family food. Use high quality frozen, packaged, and canned products to make this delicious dessert. It's fine to simplify life.

1 box (15 oz.) refrigerated pie crusts,* softened
2 containers (6 oz. each) thick and creamy crème caramel yogurt
1 package (3 oz.) cream cheese, softened
1 can (21 oz.) apple pie filling
3 tablespoons purchased caramel ice cream topping

Place 1 crust in center of large cookie sheet; place second crust directly over the first crust, matching edges and pressing to seal. Roll out into 14 inch round. Tuck ½ inch of crust edge under; flute edge. Prick crust with fork. Bake. Temperature 375°F. Time: 20 to 25 minutes or until golden brown. Cool complete, about 25 to 30 minutes. In medium bowl, beat yogurt and cream cheese together on medium speed until well-blended; spread evenly over cooled baked crust. Spread pie filling evenly over yogurt mixture; drizzle caramel topping over top. Refrigerate 2 to 3 hours before serving. A delightful change from the typical apple pie, this is an excellent dessert with its layer of creamy yogurt mixture under the apples then drizzled with a caramel topping.

2-Crust Banana Pie

Yield: 8 to 10 servings

This alternative to the Banana Cream Pie is a local favorite, although hard to find in commercial bakeries. It is still sold at Flamingo Restaurant. For true banana lovers, it's the best way to enjoy a banana dessert.

4 cups sliced firm-ripe bananas
½ cup pineapple juice
½ cup sugar
1 teaspoon cinnamon
2 tablespoons butter or margarine
Pastry for two crust pie

Soak sliced bananas in pineapple juice for 20 to 30 minutes; drain, reserving the pineapple juice. Combine bananas, sugar, cinnamon and 2 tablespoons reserved pineapple juice; toss to mix together. Pour mixture into pastry lined pie plate; dot with butter and cover with top crust. Bake at 400°F for 30 to 45 minutes or until crust is golden brown.

DESSERTS

Desserts are delicious and satisfying endings to any meal and can range from fresh fruit, to sorbet, to an elaborate souffle. They are usually sweets that go beyond cakes, pies, cookies and candies.

A few easy-to-make desserts are included for your dining pleasure.

Ice Cake

Yield: about 1 dozen cups

Before the days of flavored ices which are available today, ice cake was one of the favorite snacks for youngsters—especially on hot summer days. They were not only made at home but also sold at the neighborhood stores.

4½ cups water
1½ cups sugar
1 can (12 oz.) evaporated milk
1½ teaspoons flavor extract
1 teaspoon food coloring

Combine sugar and water in saucepan and bring to a boil; reduce heat and simmer until sugar dissolves. Add remaining ingredients; stir to combine thoroughly and pour into 4 oz. cups or ice trays and freeze.

VARIATIONS:
- Banana or lemon extract and yellow food coloring
- Mint extract with green food coloring
- Vanilla extract and no food coloring
- Vanilla extract and red food coloring

Malassadas

Yield: about 2 dozen

Few people made the famous Portuguese donuts at home, but were (and are) bakery favorites and usually made to be sold as country fair food and festa treats. These ultra rich donuts are not difficult to make and are delicious.

1 cup milk, scalded
1 package active dry yeast
3 cups flour
½ teaspoon salt
½ cup sugar
4 eggs
½ teaspoon lemon extract

Dissolve yeast in milk cooled to lukewarm. Sift dry ingredients together. Beat eggs until thick and lemon-colored. Add lemon extract and milk mixture to beaten eggs. Mix thoroughly. Stir in dry ingredients. Mix thoroughly. Cover the bowl and let stand to rise for about two hours. Drop by spoonfuls into fat heated to 365°F and fry until golden brown. Drain and roll gently in sugar.

Vanilla Chiffon Cream

Yield: 4 servings

This is a great basic recipe for a relatively inexpensive dessert. It is fluffy and looks quite elegant—besides, there are a number of variations for you to try.

1 envelope unflavored gelatin
2 tablespoons sugar
Dash of salt
2 eggs, separated
1¾ cups milk
1½ teaspoons vanilla
¼ cup sugar

Combine gelatin, sugar and salt in saucepan. Beat egg yolks with milk; stir into gelatin mixture slowly. Cook over low heat, stirring constantly, until gelatin dissolves and mixture thickens slightly, about 5 minutes. Stir in vanilla. Chill, stirring occasionally, until mixture is thickened and mounds slightly when dropped from spoon.

Beat egg whites until soft peaks form; add remaining sugar, 1 tablespoon at a time, until stiff peaks form. Fold gelatin mixture into beaten egg whites. Spoon into individual dishes. Chill until set, about 4 hours.

VARIATIONS:
Yield: 6 to 8 servings
- Chocolate Chiffon Cream: Mix ¼ cup unsweetened cocoa with gelatin, sugar and salt.

- Coffee Chiffon Cream: Substitute ½ teaspoon almond extract for vanilla; add 2 tablespoons instant coffee to gelatin, sugar and salt.

- Lemon Chiffon Cream: Substitute 2 teaspoons grated lemon rind and 2 tablespoons lemon juice for vanilla.

- Peppermint Chiffon Cream: Substitute ¼ teaspoon peppermint extract for vanilla; add few drops red food coloring.

- Chiffon Cream Pies: Pour desired chiffon cream into baked 8-inch pie shell. Top with sweetened dessert topping or sweetened whipped cream.

TIP:
If a gelatin mixture has become too firm to fold into other ingredients, set bowl of gelatin in a pan of warm water until mixture is of desired consistency.

Bavarian Cream

Yield: 6 to 8 servings

Bavarian cream desserts are easy to make and the finished product can be very elegant.

1 package (3 oz.) flavored gelatin
2 tablespoons sugar
1 cup boiling water
½ cup cold water or fruit juice
1 envelope dessert topping mix or 1 cup whipping cream

Dissolve gelatin and sugar in boiling water. Add cold water. Chill until slightly thickened. Prepare dessert topping mix as directed on package or whip the cream until stiff; stir 1½ cups into gelatin until blended. Pour into 1-quart mold or 6 to 8 individual serving dishes. Chill until firm, about 4 hours. To serve, top with remaining dessert topping or sweetened whipped cream.

VARIATIONS:

- Fruit Bavarians: Fold into Bavarian Cream before chilling, 1 cup sliced or diced fresh or drained canned fruit.

- Angel Delight: Break one-half angel food cake into bite-sized pieces. Arrange in alternate layers with Bavarian Cream in angel food cake pan.

- Bavarian Cream Pie: Pour Bavarian Cream into baked 8-inch pie shell.

Broken Glass Gelatin

Yield: 20 to 24 servings

Here's a colorful, delicious summer dessert! It's the perfect dessert for hot summer meals as it's also refreshing.

5 boxes (3 oz. each) flavored gelatin, different flavors
5 cups hot water
7 packets plain gelatin
3 cups warm skim milk
1 cup sugar
Sweetened whipped cream, optional

Separately dissolve each box of flavored gelatin with 1 cup hot water; add ½ packet of plain gelatin to each mixture. Mix each until completely dissolved; refrigerate until firm.

In separate bowl, mix warm skim milk with sugar and 4 packets plain gelatin; mix until completely dissolved; let cool to room temperature. Slice each chilled flavored gelatin into cubes or desired shapes and sizes; arrange in greased 9 x 13-Inch pan. Pour cooled milk mixture over flavored gelatin pieces; refrigerate until firm. Serve with sweetened whipped cream, if desired.

Old Fashioned Bread Pudding

Yield: 12 servings

Bread pudding is so delicious considering the fact that it's made from leftover bread. It is a humble dessert but it can also be decadent with add-ins and flavorings. The variations are endless—that's part of the fun of making it. Use the basic recipe and create a comforting treat or jazz it up for a richer dessert fit to suit your guests.

6 eggs, slightly beaten
1 cup sugar
½ teaspoon salt
6 cups half-and-half or milk*
2 teaspoons vanilla
Custard flavoring of choice (on next page)
10 cups 1-inch day old bread cubes (see Bread Choices on next page)
Add-ins (see next page), optional
½ cup butter or margarine
*Evaporated milk diluted with water may be substituted for half-and-half or milk.

In large heatproof bowl, whisk eggs with sugar and salt until thoroughly combined; set aside.

Heat half-and-half or milk in medium saucepan over medium heat until steaming but not bubbling. Slowly whisk the half-and-half or milk into the egg mixture until thoroughly combined; strain mixture through sieve into large heatproof bowl. Add vanilla. Put the bread cubes in 9 x 13-inch baking dish and pour custard on top; make sure the bread is submerged in the custard and let cool at room temperature, about 35 minutes. Cover with plastic wrap and refrigerate for 6 hours or overnight.

If you'd like to include add-ins, transfer the bread mixture to a large mixing bowl and gently fold in the add-ins just before baking. Return mixture to the baking dish; dot with butter on top. Cover loosely with foil. Bake. 325°F. Time: to 70 minutes. Remove foil and continue to bake until no liquid custard is visible when pudding is poked in the center with a paring knife, about 20 to 40 additional minutes or until golden brown. Cool few minutes. Serve warm, at room temperature or chilled with your favorite vanilla sauce, dollop of sweetened whipped cream or ice cream.

VARIATIONS:

Add-ins: BREAD CHOICES (10 CUPS)
Brioche, Challah, Croissant, French, Whole Wheat, White

OPTIONAL FLAVORINGS (Choose 1)

Almond—add 1½ teaspoons
Chocolate—add 2 cups chopped bittersweet chocolate to hot milk; whisk to melt
Coffee—add 2 teaspoons instant espresso powder to hot milk; whisk to dissolve
Lemon—add finely grated zest of 3 lemons to milk before heating; whisk ½ cup lemon juice into custard
Pumpkin—whisk 1½ cups canned pumpkin, 1 teaspoon ground cinnamon and ½ teaspoon grated nutmeg into custard

OPTIONAL ADD-INS (Choose 1 or 2)

3 bananas, thinly sliced
3½ cups fresh or frozen berries
1½ cups toasted coarsely chopped nuts
1 cup chopped semi-sweet or bittersweet chocolate
1 cup chopped dried apricots, soak in hot water and drained
1 cup raisins, soaked in hot water and drained

Strawberry Fluff Parfait

Yield: 6 to 8 servings

Our thanks to Charles Knox for these refreshing parfait desserts. He invented the quintessential gelatin, the primary ingredient for this dessert, in 1894.

2 packages (3 oz. each) strawberry flavored gelatin
1 pint strawberry ice cream
2 cups boiling water
1 package (10 oz.) frozen strawberries, thawed

Dissolve gelatin in boiling water; add ice cream and stir until thoroughly combined. Chill until slightly congealed, then beat until fluffy. Add strawberries and mix. Spoon into parfait glasses and chill.

VARIATIONS: Mix 'n Match Parfaits (Prepare as directed above.)

GELATIN	FROZEN DESSERT	FRUIT
Raspberry gelatin	1 pint raspberry sherbet	1 package (10 oz.) frozen cranberryorange relish, thawed
Orange gelatin	1 pint orange sherbet	1 can (11 oz.) mandarin oranges (undrained)
Lime gelatin	1 pint lime sherbet	1 can (8 oz.) apple sauce
Lemon gelatin	1 pint lemon sherbet	1 can (8¾ oz.) crushed pineapple, undrained
Raspberry gelatin	1 pint raspberry sherbet	1 package (10 oz.) frozen raspberries, thawed

Strawberry Shortcake

Yield: 12 servings

This is a great basic recipe for a relatively inexpensive dessert. It is fluffy and looks quite elegant—besides, there are a number of variations for you to try.

1 pint vanilla ice cream, softened (but thick)
2 cups prepared Basic Biscuit Mix (see page 22)
4 cups sweetened strawberries
2 cups heavy cream, whipped

Add ice cream to biscuit mix and mix only until dry ingredients are moistened.
Fill greased muffin pans (1¾ x 1 inch) about ⅔ full. Bake in a preheated 425°F oven about 15 minutes. Remove from pan and cool about 10 minutes; split. Allow one cake for each serving. Top halves with fruit and whipped cream.

VARIATIONS: Mix 'n Match Rainbow Shortcakes using the following combinations.
Prepare as directed for Strawberry Shortcake above.

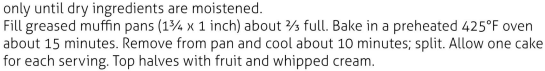

FROZEN DESSERT	FRUIT
1 pint raspberry sherbet	4 cups raspberries
1 pint butter pecan ice cream	4 cups sliced peaches
1 pint lemon sherbet	4 cups blueberries

Appendices

WEIGHTS AND MEASURES	
Dash	Less than ⅛ teaspoon
1 tablespoon	3 teaspoons/14.8 milliliters
4 tablespoons	¼ cup
5⅓ tablespoons	⅓ cup
8 tablespoons	½ cup
12 tablespoons	¾ cup
16 tablespoons	1 cup/2 gills/8 fluid ounces
1 fluid ounce	2 tablespoons
1 cup	½ pint (liquid)
2 cups	1 pint
2 pints	4 cups/1 quart/946.4 milliliters
4 quarts	1 gallon
8 quarts	1 peck (dry)
4 pecks	1 bushel
16 ounces	1 pound/453.59 grains
1 teaspoon	4.9 milliliters
1 liter	1000 milliliters/1.06 quarts
1 ounce	28.35 grams
1 gram	0.035 ounces
1 kilogram	2.21 pounds

SEASONAL CHART

MONTH	FRUITS & VEGETABLES	OTHERS
JAN	Fresh oranges and orange products · Fresh grapefruit · Canned and fresh pears · Apples · Canned tomatoes and tomato products · Dry beans, lentils, dry peas	Broiler-Fryers
FEB	Apples · Potatoes · Grapefruit · Canned and frozen corn · Oranges and orange products · Canned tomatoes and tomato products	Broiler-Fryers
MARCH	Canned pears · Canned and frozen corn · Canned tomatoes and tomato products	Rice · Broiler-Fryer · Peanuts and peanut products
APRIL	Dry beans · Applesauces · Canned peaches · Canned and frozen corn · Canned tomato products · Mango	Honey · Eggs · Peanut and peanut products
MAY	Canned tomato products · Canned fruit cocktail · Canned and frozen corn · Canned green beans · Canned applesauce · Dry split peas · Mango · Papaya	Milk and dairy products · Eggs
JUNE	Guava · Pineapple · Mango · Lychee · Passion fruit · Papaya	Milk and dairy products · Honey · Eggs
JULY	Fresh sweet corn · Carrots · Leafy greens · Breadfruit · Guava · Pineapple · Mango · Lychee · Passion fruit	Broiler-Fryers
AUGUST	Summer vegetables · Watermelons · Fresh plums · Breadfruit · Guava · Pineapple · Passion fruit · Mango	Wheat products · Peanut and peanut products
SEPT	Canned peaches · Canned applesauce · Dry split peas · Fresh pears · Fresh limes · Guava · Mango · Passion fruit	Peanut and peanut products
OCT	Dry split peas · Apples · Pears · Canned peaches · Potatoes · Breadfruit · Guava · Papaya	Broiler-Fryers · Rice
NOV	Canned and frozen green beans · Canned peaches · Sweet potatoes · Dry beans · Potatoes · Apples · Papaya	Broiler-Fryers · Turkeys · Rice
DEC	Canned tomatoes and tomato products · Dry beans · Split peas and lentils · Sweet potatoes · Canned peaches · Fresh and canned pears · Potatoes · Apples	Broiler-Fryers

MEAT AND POULTRY STORAGE TIME

MEAT

Refrigerator (38°F to 40°F)	Meat	Freezer (0°F or lower)
2 to 4 days	Beef (fresh)	6 to 12 months
2 to 4 days	Veal (fresh)	6 to 9 months
2 to 4 days	Pork (fresh)	3 to 6 months
2 to 4 days	Lamb (fresh)	6 to 9 months
1 to 2 days	Ground beef, veal and lamb	3 to 4 months
1 to 2 days	Ground pork	1 to 3 months
1 to 2 days	Variety meats	3 to 4 months
1 week	Luncheon meats	
2 to 3 days	Sausage, fresh pork	
3 to 7 days	Sausage, smoked	
2 to 3 weeks	Sausage, dry and semi-dry (unsliced)	
4 to 5 days	Frankfurters	2 weeks
5 to 7 days	Bacon	2 weeks
7 days	Smoked ham, whole	2 months
3 to 4 days	Smoked ham, slices	
1 week	Beef, corned	2 weeks
4 to 5 days	Leftover cooked meat	2 to 3 months

FROZEN COMBINATION FOODS

Refrigerator (38°F to 40°F)	Frozen Combination Foods	Freezer (0°F or lower)
	Meat pies, cooked	3 months
	Swiss steak, cooked	3 months
	Stews, cooked	3 to 4 months
	Prepared meat dinners	2 to 6 months

RAW POULTRY

Refrigerator (38°F to 40°F)	Raw Poultry	Freezer (0°F or lower)
	Chicken and turkey	12 months
	Duck, goose	6 months
	Cooked poultry dishes	6 months
	Fried chicken	4 months

Healthy Diet Guidelines

EAT A VARIETY OF FOODS
- Fruits and Vegetables
- Whole grain and enriched breads, cereals and grain products milk,cheese and yogurt
- Meats, poultry, fish and eggs
- Legumes (dried peas and beans)

MAINTAIN AN IDEAL WEIGHT
Obesity is a risk factor for many diseases including heart disease, high blood pressure, diabetes, and some cancers.

AVOID EXCESSIVE FAT, SATURATED FAT AND CHOLESTEROL
- Choose lean meat, fish, poultry, dry beans and peas as your protein sources.
- Moderate use of eggs and organ meats.
- Limit intake of butter, cream, hydrogenated margarine, shortenings and coconuts oil and foods made from such products.
- Trim excess fat off meats. Bake, broil or boil rather than fry.
- Read labels carefully to determine amount and types of fat in foods.

EAT FOODS WITH ADEQUATE STARCH AND FIBER
Eat foods with adequate fiber to reduce cholesterol and glucose absorption in the gastrointestinol system—fiber also reduces risk of diverticulosis symptoms and risk of colon and rectal cancer.

AVOID EXCESSIVE SUGAR
- A diet high in sugar promotes tooth decay. Sugary foods are also often high in fat and calories and low in vitamins and minerals.
- Use less of all sugars and eat less of foods containing sugars—i.e. candy, soft drinks, cakes, etc.
- Read food labels for sugar content.

AVOID EXCESSIVE SALT AND SODIUM
- Too much sodium in the diet may contribute to high blood pressure, especially for people with a family history of high blood pressure. Untreated high blood pressure can lead to heart attacks, strokes and kidney disease.
- Learn to enjoy the natural,unsalted flavors of foods.
- Use only small amounts of salt in cooking or at the table.
- Limit your intake of salty foods— i.e. chips, pickled foods, cured meats, condiments (soy sauce, garlic salt, etc.)

AVOID EXCESSIVE ALCOHOL
Heavy drinking is associated with cancers of the mouth, throat, esophagus and liver. Cancer risk is especlally high for heavy drinkers who smoke. Alcohol also reduces fat digestion causing increased amounts of cholesterol and triglycerides in the blood. In addition, alcoholic drinks are high in calories and low in vitamins and minerals.

Glossary

'Ahi – Hawaiian name for yellowfin tuna

Aku – Hawaiian name for skipjack tuna

Bibimbap – Korean-style mixed rice

Char siu – Chinese sweet roasted pork

Chawan mushi – Japanese-style egg custard

Chinese five-spice powder – blend of star anise, cloves, fennel, peppercorns and cinnamon

Chinese parsley – cilantro

Chop chae – Korean fried noodles

Chow fun – Chinese dish; stir-fried flat rice noodles

Chow mein noodles – Chinese soft-fried wheat or egg noodles

Coconut milk – juice from meat of coconut

Dashi konbu – kelp used for soup stock

Dashi-no-moto – Japanese instant soup stock granules

Furikake – Japanese seasoned seaweed mix

Gau gee – crispy deep-fried Chinese dumpling filled with pork

Ginger – root of the domestic ginger plant used as a seasoning both in savory dishes and sweet (powdered ginger is not a good substitute)

Gobo – Japanese for burdock root

Gon lo mein – stir fried chow mein noodles

Guava – thin-skinned fruit with a sweet or slightly acid pulp

Hawaiian red pepper – small, hot, red chili pepper

Hawaiian salt – coarse sea salt

Hoisin sauce – Chinese soybean sauce used as a condiment or for flavoring

Jook – Chinese rice soup; aka congee

Kalbi – Korean barbecued short ribs

Kalua – Hawaiian method of cooking food in an underground pit called "imu"

Kamaboko – Japanese steamed fish cake

Katsu – Japanese word for "cutlet"

Kim chee – peppery pickled vegetables

Kizami nori – shredded seaweed

Kumu – red goat fish

Lavosh – crisp Armenian flat bread

Li hing mui – Chinese dried preserved fruit

Liliko'i – Hawaiian name for passion fruit

Long rice – translucent noodles made from mung beans

Mahimahi – dolfinfish

Mango – gold and green tropical fruit

Maui onion – sweet onions grown on Maui

Mirin – Japanese sweet rice wine

Miso – fermented Japanese soybean paste

Misoyaki – Japanese dish; meat or fish marinated in miso then broiled

Mochi – glutinous Japanese rice cakes

Mochiko – Japanese name for glutinous rice flour

Monosodium glutamate (MSG) – flavor enhancer

Musubi – rice ball

Namasu – Japanese pickled vegetable dish

Nori – Japanese name for dried purple seaweed sheets; laver

Nuoc mam – Vietnamese fish sauce

Orange peel (kwo kee) – orange-brown dried rind of various fruits used to give a distinctive citrus flavor to soups and meats

Oyster sauce – Chinese oyster-flavored sauce

Panko – Japanese flour meal for breading

Passion fruit – egg-shaped fruit with seedy pulp and tough skin; aka liliko'i

Poke – Hawaiian seafood appetizer

Portuguese sausage – garlic and pepper-flavored pork sausage; linguisa

Sake – Japanese rice wine

Salsa – spicy, hot Mexican condiment made of red or green chilis

Shichimi togarashi – seven flavors spice; blend of pepper leaf, poppy seed, rape seed, hemp seed, dried tangerine peel, and sesame seed

Shiitake – dried mushrooms

Shirataki – Japanese gelatinous noodle-like strips made from tuberous root flour

Shoyu – soy sauce

Somen – thin, Japanese wheat flour noodles

Star anise – a highly fragrant dried spice that looks like a star and tastes like anise

Sushi – Japanese vinegar flavored rice

Teriyaki – Japanese soy-flavored sauce

Tofu – Japanese name for soybean curd

Won ton wrappers – thin squares of dough used to make dumplings

Yakitori – Japanese for broiled chicken

Index

O

oat cereal
Hawaiian Jambles, 6

oatmeal
Oatmeal Cookies, 113

Okinawan
An Da Gi, 112
Rafute, 62

oxtail
Kari Kari, 136
Oven Braised Oxtail Stew, 137
Oxtail Peanut Soup, 131

P

papaya, green
Tinola, 136

peanuts
Boiled Peanuts, 14
Chinese Chicken Salad, 123
Energy Bars, 179
Kari Kari, 136
Oxtail Peanut Soup, 131
Tofu Tempura, 159

peas
Chicken Chop Suey, 161
Mix-and-Match Wikiwiki Vegetables, 162
Tamago Meshi, 142

pies
2-Crust Banana Pie, 191
Caramel Apple Tarts, 191
Coconut Cream Pie, 190
Custard Pie, 185
Fresh Strawberry Pie, 189
Guava Chiffon Pie, 190
Fluffy Key Lime Pie, 187
Pumpkin Chiffon Pie, 188

pineapple juice
2-Crust Banana Pie, 191

Pineapple Upside Down Cake, 176
Sweet-Sour Spareribs, 60
Tropical Carrot Cake, 172

poi
Taro Stew, 139

pork
Adobo, 50
Baked Hoisin Barbecue Ribs, 55
Barbecued Cantonese Ribs, 53
Carne De Vinha D'Alhos, 59
Char Siu, 56
Classic Fried Rice, 87
Crispy Roast Pork, 61
Egg Foo Yong, 142
Haole Laulau, 57
Hot and Sour Soup, 128
Kim Chee Soup, 132
Korean-Style Fried Rice, 91
Oven Kalua Pork, 57
Pansit, 98
Pork Tofu, 55
Rafute, 62
Roast Pork Loin, 52
Szechwan Eggplant, 157

pork, ground
Bacon-Wrapped Meat Loaf, 45
Gau Gee with Sweet and Sour Sauce, 6
Gyoza, 11
Spanish Rice, 90

Portuguese
Carne De Vinha D'Alhos, 59
Malassadas, 193
Portuguese Bean Soup, 129
Portuguese Sweet Bread, 25

potato
Beef Vegetable Soup, 129
Kim Chee Soup, 132
Macaroni-Potato Salad, 118

Oven Braised Oxtail Stew, 137
Oven Pot Roast, 38
Portuguese Bean Soup, 129
potato, 134

prune
Prune Cake, 171
Prune Frosting, 171
Prune Mui, 109

pumpkin
Pumpkin Chiffon Pie, 188

R

radish
Cucumber Namasu, 106

raisins
Energy Bars, 179

rice
Bibimbap, 91
Jook, 131
Korean-Style Fried Rice, 91
Oyako Donburi, 147
Spanish Rice, 90
Sushi Rice, 89
Tamago Meshi, 142
Teriyaki Spam™ Musubi, 109

rice cereal
Energy Bars, 179
Hawaiian Jambles, 6

rice noodles
Pansit, 98

rice sticks
Pho, 101

round steak
Swiss Steak, 36

rump roast
Oven Pot Roast, 38

About the Author

Muriel Miura may be most recognized for her 1970s nationally televised cooking shows, *Cook Japanese Hawaiian Style* and *The New World of Cooking with Muriel*. (She was the first local chef to have her own TV program and the first woman in Hawai'i to have a TV show.) While comfortable with all types of cuisine, Muriel's specialty was Japanese cooking where she added a personal touch of Hawai'i to her dishes.

Muriel was a prolific author, writing more than twenty-five cookbooks including *Cookies from Hawai'i's Kitchen*, *Hawai'i Cooks with Spam*, *Hawai'i Cooks and Saves*, *Celebrating in Hawai'i*, *What Hawai'i Likes to Eat*, and *A Japanese Kitchen*. She also served as co-editor of the "Hawai'i Cooks" series that featuring *A Korean Kitchen*, *A Portuguese Kitchen*, *An Okinawan Kitchen*, *A Chinese Kitchen*, and *A Filipino Kitchen*. A book on dim sum with Lynette Lo Tom is scheduled for release.

Throughout her culinary career, she judged food contests, taught community cooking classes and high school home economics, wrote articles about cuisine and food, and traveled to the New York World's Fair as a featured presenter where she won a prestigious award for outstanding demonstration. Muriel also guest-starred on the popular *Hari's Kitchen TV* cooking show.

Muriel graduated from the University of Hawai'i's Home Economics program and earned graduate degrees in Home Economics Education from the University of Hawai'i at Mānoa and Columbia University of New York City. She was the director of Home Economics at The Gas Company until 1993. Following her retirement, besides writing cookbooks, she was involved with a number of community service projects and served on the Board of Directors and Board of Trustees of the Mō'ili'ili Community Center.